Richard Nisbet
Abbotsneuk
March street
Peebles
Peebleshire

Richard Nisbet
Abbotsneuk

Flight

Peter Shephard

Flight

Ward Lock Limited · London

© Ward Lock Limited 1976

ISBN 0 7063 1860 9

First published in Great Britain 1976
by Ward Lock Limited, 116 Baker
Street, London, W1M 2BB, a member
of the Pentos Group

Designed by Grant Gibson

Text filmset in Century Schoolbook
by Servis Filmsetting Limited,
Manchester

Printed and bound by
Toppan Printing Company,
Singapore

Contents

ACKNOWLEDGMENTS

The Publishers wish to thank John
Young for executing the artwork,
and also the undermentioned sources
for permission to reproduce
illustrations used in this book:
Janet and Colin Bord; British
Aircraft Corporation; British
Airports Authority; Flight
International; Fox Photos; Arthur
Gibson; Hawker-Siddeley; Lockheed;
Ministry of Defence; Rolls-Royce;
Peter Shephard

International airports

One of the best ways of seeing aeroplanes at close quarters is to visit a big international airport like London's Heathrow.

London Airport is the most important air travel centre in the world. On busy days in summer as many as seventy-eight aircraft arrive and depart every hour. The greatest number of aircraft movements so far recorded for any one day was 984. The total of passengers handled in a day can exceed 75,000 people.

The aeroplane long ago overtook the ocean liner as the principle means of international travel. In Britain less than thirty per cent of overseas journeys now begin or end at sea ports.

Even on the slackest day in mid-winter there are at least 500 movements at Heathrow, so the visitor will always find something exciting to watch. The aircraft may be in the colours of any one of the sixty airlines that use the airport. In addition there are executive jets and helicopters, plus an occasional military machine.

Civil airports are not concerned only with passenger transport. Air freight is a fast-growing industry. Heathrow is Britain's third largest port, after London and Liverpool. In terms of the value of freight shifted, the cargo aeroplane is beginning to rival the cargo ship. Giant flying freighters now on the drawing board will dwarf the Jumbo jet, just as the Jumbo dwarfs the 707s and VC10s today.

Heathrow has one of the largest cargo terminals in the world. It occupies 160 acres and handles well over half a million tons of freight every year. There are thirty stands to accommodate the largest aircraft. Cargo handling is fully automated and all movements are planned by computer.

London Airport welcomes spectators. Visitors are able to get a splendid view from the roof garden above Queen's Building and from the roof of Number 2 Terminal. The roof gardens are open from 10.00 hours throughout the year with the exception of Christmas Day and Boxing Day. Entry charge is 16p for adults and 6p for children.

The view covers some two-thirds of the airport. The whole of Number 5 runway and the eastern end of Number 1 runway can be seen. A running commentary is broadcast over the public address system giving details of incoming and outgoing flights. Pay telescopes are provided at intervals. These allow keen spotters to pick up and identify aircraft five miles (8km) out on the glide path.

The roof gardens have shops selling magazines and model kits. There is a licensed café, tuck shops and ice cream stalls. If a younger brother or sister tires of aeroplanes there is a well-equipped children's playground which will keep them occupied for hours.

Visitors are welcome to use

binoculars, telescopes and cameras. Film is on sale in the roof shops. The only restriction is on the use of tripods which might cause accidents.

There are many points of interest in addition to the aircraft themselves. To the north and south of Queen's Building can be seen the piers and aircraft stands of Terminals 1 and 2. These handle domestic and short-haul international flights. Over to the west is No.3 – the long-haul Terminal – with its many stands for the Jumbo jets. Immediately in front of Queen's Building is the Control Tower with its cupola of green tinted glass.

On the upper floors of this building sit the air traffic controllers. These are the men and women who have the awesome responsibility of guiding airliners safely in and out of Heathrow.

'Approach Control' operators sit in near darkness. Their radar screens show the airliners as moving blips which leave a short trail. In the centre of the screen is a diagrammatic image of the airport with its runways.

The controllers bring the aircraft in to intersect with the beams of the Instrument Landing System (ILS). In busy periods the incoming aircraft may have to queue. This is done in 'stacks' to the north and south of the field. The waiting aeroplane enters the stack at 25,000 to 30,000 feet (7,500–9,000m) and orbits. Aircraft move down the stack as aircraft at the bottom are brought in to land.

The minimum height over London is 3,000 feet (900m) to reduce noise nuisance. When an aircraft is established on the Instrument Landing System, the radar controller hands over to the visual controller in the cupola. The visual controller is responsible for final approach, touchdown and movement to the aircraft parking stand.

Spacing between aircraft on final approach depends on prevailing weather conditions. In good visibility the interval may be as little as three miles (4.8km). In bad weather the gap may increase to six miles (9.6km).

Should a pilot declare an emergency he receives priority over all other traffic. Emergency services, including the very latest rescue and fire fighting equipment, race to their predetermined stations beside the runway. In bad visibility all ground movement of vehicles and aircraft can be monitored on the special ground surveillance radar. This is so sensitive that it once pinpointed a stray horse which had broken loose and bolted.

The best way to visit London Airport is to travel by public transport. A number of London Transport and Greenline bus services run into Airport Central. Others pass the airfield on the north side. The Piccadilly Underground service runs to nearby Hounslow West, and will soon continue to the airport itself. British Rail serve Feltham Station.

Bus services link both stations with Airport Central.

Visitors arriving by car should approach on the A4 (Bath Road), which passes the north side of the field, or on the M4 motorway. A spur of the M4 links directly with Airport Central.

Spectators should leave their cars in the Spectators' Car Park on the north side. In the summer months a regular bus shuttle links this car park with the central area.

Aéroport Charles de Gaulle

Across the channel, near Paris, is the world's newest international airport. Scarcely forty minutes flying time from Heathrow, Aéroport Charles de Gaulle is twenty-five miles (40km) north-west of the centre of Paris. It was opened in March 1974 and it is expected to be handling 40,000,000 passengers a year by the 80s.

The central terminal building is circular. The upper storeys provide parking space for thousands of cars. Around the terminal are seven 'island' sub-terminals which are

left top: *layout of runways and terminal buildings;* centre: *the check-in desks;* below: *moveable corridors link terminal and aircraft*

reached by underground moving pavements or travelators. The sub-terminals allow up to forty aircraft to be handled at any one time.

In planning the passenger handling facilities the designers have borne in mind the probability that the airbuses of the 80s will seat 1,000 or more passengers. Everything possible has been done to reduce delays for passengers. Walking distance between road transport and aircraft has been halved in comparison with Orly – the other Paris Airport.

When it opened, Charles de Gaulle had only one runway. When the airport is completed in 1990 it will have five runways. Additional terminals will be added to cope with the ever growing passenger load. The new airport is also designed to cope with the great expansion of air freight services that is anticipated in the immediate future.

Perhaps the most visually striking feature of Aéroport Charles de Gaulle is the control tower. Supported on a slender column, it soars some 80 metres or 267 feet above the airfield, giving a magnificent panoramic view over the central terminal to the runway beyond.

right top *view from the control tower at Heathrow Airport;* centre: *radar plays an important part in monitoring aircraft movements;* below: *fire engines and ambulances are always on stand-by for emergency;* bottom: *No. 7 Pier at Heathrow, used by 747 'Jumbos'. The 300m corridor, with two moving passenger walkways, links the waiting-rooms and terminal building*

From Boxkite to MRCA

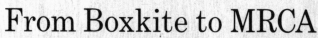

Little more than seventy years – a single human life span – separates the Boxkite from the Panavia MRCA. In the intervening years a multitude of aircraft types of every shape and size were built and flown. Some were successful while others failed. Each one was to be outdated and superseded within a period of a few months or a few years.

On this and the following pages we shall look at some of the successes.

The Boxkite of 1913 was little more than a refined version of the Wright Flyer with wheels in place of skids

represented here by a Royal Navy 'North Sea' class ship, was seen as the aerial transport of the future. Count Ferdinand von Zeppelin showed the way in the years between 1910 and 1914 when his great silver ships carried thousands of passengers safely on scheduled air services. When the First World War ended in 1918, the airship seemed certain to rule the air lanes, but a series of disasters brought the airship story to

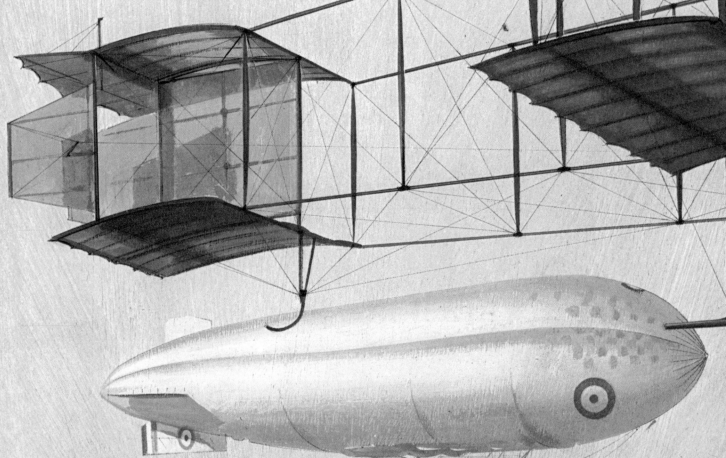

and moveable control surfaces in place of the Wright method of wing warping. The Boxkite, a replica of which can be seen at Shuttleworth Trust displays, trained many of the airmen who later flew Camels, Pups and SE5As over the battlefields of France.

In the early days of flying no one believed that the aeroplane would ever carry worthwhile loads over great distances. The airship,

a close. Today, with new techniques and non-explosive helium to provide lift, it is possible that giant airships may once again be seen sailing silently across the skies.

In contrast to the ungainly Boxkite, the dainty Hawker Fury was perhaps the most beautiful of all the biplane fighters. Designed by Sidney Camm, who later created the Hurricane, Typhoon and Harrier, the

Demon served with RAF squadrons in the 30s and performed thrilling displays of aerobatics at the pre-war Air Pageants at Hendon in north London.

Some aircraft reveal their ancestry in every line. The Supermarine Walrus was a direct descendant of the flying boat racers which carried Britain's colours in the

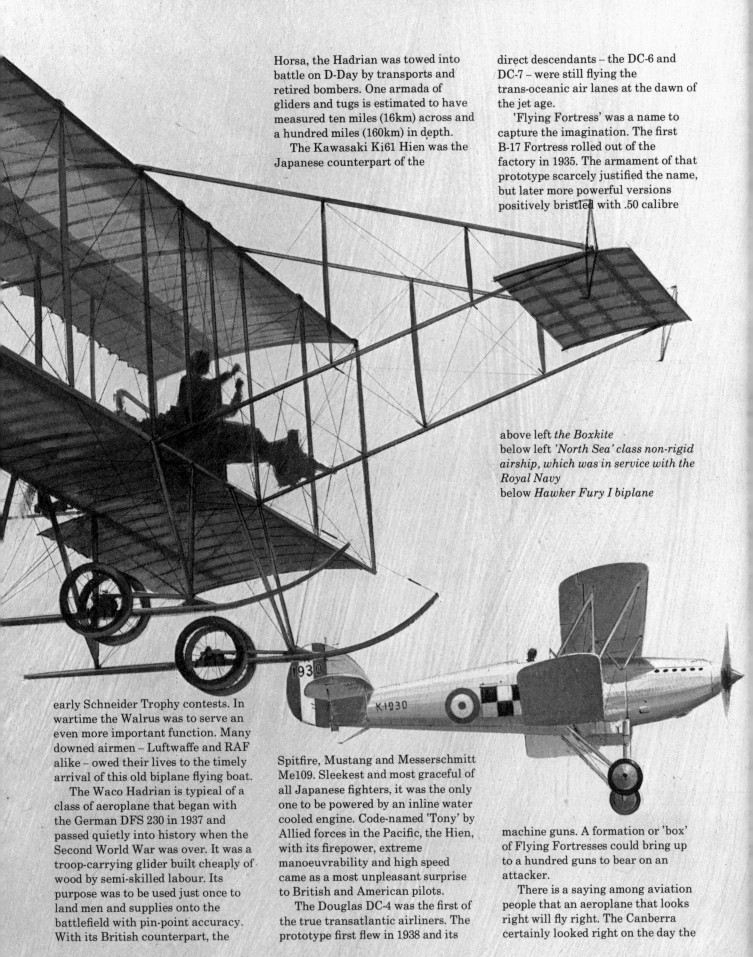

Horsa, the Hadrian was towed into battle on D-Day by transports and retired bombers. One armada of gliders and tugs is estimated to have measured ten miles (16km) across and a hundred miles (160km) in depth.

The Kawasaki Ki61 Hien was the Japanese counterpart of the

direct descendants – the DC-6 and DC-7 – were still flying the trans-oceanic air lanes at the dawn of the jet age.

'Flying Fortress' was a name to capture the imagination. The first B-17 Fortress rolled out of the factory in 1935. The armament of that prototype scarcely justified the name, but later more powerful versions positively bristled with .50 calibre

above left *the Boxkite*
below left *'North Sea' class non-rigid airship, which was in service with the Royal Navy*
below *Hawker Fury I biplane*

early Schneider Trophy contests. In wartime the Walrus was to serve an even more important function. Many downed airmen – Luftwaffe and RAF alike – owed their lives to the timely arrival of this old biplane flying boat.

The Waco Hadrian is typical of a class of aeroplane that began with the German DFS 230 in 1937 and passed quietly into history when the Second World War was over. It was a troop-carrying glider built cheaply of wood by semi-skilled labour. Its purpose was to be used just once to land men and supplies onto the battlefield with pin-point accuracy. With its British counterpart, the

Spitfire, Mustang and Messerschmitt Me109. Sleekest and most graceful of all Japanese fighters, it was the only one to be powered by an inline water cooled engine. Code-named 'Tony' by Allied forces in the Pacific, the Hien, with its firepower, extreme manoeuvrability and high speed came as a most unpleasant surprise to British and American pilots.

The Douglas DC-4 was the first of the true transatlantic airliners. The prototype first flew in 1938 and its

machine guns. A formation or 'box' of Flying Fortresses could bring up to a hundred guns to bear on an attacker.

There is a saying among aviation people that an aeroplane that looks right will fly right. The Canberra certainly looked right on the day the

right *Supermarine Walrus biplane flying boat*
centre *English Electric Canberra, the first practical jet bomber*
bottom *Waco CG-4A Hadrian, a troop carrying glider made of wood*

FUERZA AEREA ARGENTINA

top *Kawasaki Ki61, a Japanese fighter that challenged the Allied planes*
centre *Boeing B-17 Flying Fortress bomber*
bottom *Douglas DC-4 (C-54) Skymaster, one of the first transatlantic planes*

first prototype took to the air, and in a quarter of a century of service flying it has changed only in detail.

The Canberra was the first practical jet bomber. It was ordered into large scale service with the Royal Air Force. It was also built under licence in Australia and in the United States, where it is known as the B-57. It continues in large scale service with many air forces, and reconditioned Canberras are still being produced.

The Sea Vixen was the ultimate development of the de Havilland Vampire jet fighter of 1945. Conceived originally as an all-weather fighter for the RAF, the design was 'navalized' for service aboard Royal Navy carriers. Swept wings, twin booms and a 'slab' tailplane gave the Sea Vixen a

unique appearance. It carried a crew of two, and its twin Avon turbojets made it supersonic in a shallow dive. Sea Vixens were equipped for air-to-air refuelling and could remain airborne for long periods.

The Boeing 727 is one of the most successful of subsonic jetliners. Powered by three Pratt and Whitney

turbofans, it can carry up to 189 passengers over a range of 2,000 miles (3,200km). More than a thousand Boeing 727s are in service and many more are on order.

The de Havilland Canada DHC5 Buffalo is a military short take-off and landing (STOL) aircraft. Large-diameter paddle-bladed airscrews and high-lift flaps enable the Buffalo to lift forty-one fully armed troops in and out of small unprepared airfields.

The Dassault Mirage 111E is a delta wing fighter. The delta wing is

top *de Havilland CC-115 Buffalo, a short take-off transport*
centre *Boeing 727 (AA) subsonic jetliner*
bottom *the Russian helicopter Mil Mi-6*

so-called because its shape is similar to the fourth letter of the Greek alphabet. The Mirage is one of the most successful of modern fighter designs. In the 1967 Arab-Israeli War, it dramatically demonstrated its superiority over contemporary Russian fighters. Today the Mirage is in service with ten air forces.

The conception of the rotating wing was known to the ancient Chinese, but the first really successful helicopter did not fly until 1940. Great progress has been made since then. The giant Russian Mil Mi-6 has a 34.7-metre-diameter rotor driven by two 5,500hp Solovieb turboshafts. It can lift an eleven-ton load and fly at a speed of 175mph (280km/h).

The Panavia MRCA would have seemed pure science fiction to the pilot of a Boxkite – or even to the pilot of a Flying Fortress. A 'multi-role combat aircraft' built by BAC, Messerschmitt-Bolkow-Blohm

top de Havilland Sea Vixen, which served with the Royal Navy
centre Dassault Mirage 111E, a modern delta-wing fighter
bottom Panavia 200 Tornado, a multi-role combat aircraft

(Germany) and Fiat (Italy) it can fly faster than twice the speed of sound at high altitude. At tree top height it can exceed the speed of sound with a greater bomb load than a B-17.

Modern airliners

Airliners come in many shapes and sizes. They range from small 'commuter-liners' like the Britten-Norman BN-2 Islander to huge, 'wide-body' Jumbos like the Boeing 747. Why are they all so different?

Each airliner is designed to carry out a particular job. An Islander can make a profit carrying five or six people short distances over difficult terrain. A typical example of this is the 'Highlands and Islands' service offered by the Loganair company in Scotland. Some of their flights between islands last only a minute or two, but the same journey by boat might take several hours and be highly uncomfortable. Some 600 BN-2 Islanders are in service in America, Africa, Australasia and in island communities across the Pacific.

'Tail-jet' airliners such as the Boeing 727 and the Trident Two were designed to give passengers a quieter and more comfortable ride. For this reason the engines were placed well behind the passenger cabin. This idea has been very successful. At least a dozen different tail-jet designs are in service. More than 1,100 Boeing 727s have been built, and the Trident family of jetliners is in service in many countries, including the People's Republic of China.

But fashions in airliner design change almost as quickly as fashions in clothes. Although the tail-jets will continue in service until the late 80s, they are already a part of the older generation of passenger aeroplanes. One reason for this is that they were created at a time when noise was not an important consideration in airliner design. Today there is ever mounting criticism of aircraft noise from people who live near to international airports.

Some engine manufacturers are now making 'hush-kits' to reduce the noise level of such machines as the 727 and the Trident. These devices, however, have only a limited effect and they tend to reduce the efficiency of the engine.

The answer to the noise problem is to be found in the new generation of wide-body Jumbos – the Boeing 747,

the McDonnell DC-10 and the Lockheed Tri-Star. These are the engine and airframe manufacturers' response to the demand for quieter aeroplanes. They have been referred to as the 'good neighbour' airliners. Powered by massive turbofan engines, they make far less noise and exhaust smoke than their smaller counterparts. In addition they carry three or four times the number of passengers. That means fewer landings and take-offs, still further reducing noise pollution.

Concorde is the shape of the future in civil aviation. Flying at 16,500 metres and cruising at 1,350mph (2,160km/h) it halves the normal flight time from Europe to America. It carries up to 144 people over ranges of more than 3,600 miles (5,700km).

Concorde has attracted much criticism because of noise and exhaust fumes. In fact much of the criticism is unfounded. Concorde has been proved to make less noise than a Boeing 707, and in production form it emits far less smoke than a Boeing 727 or a Convair Coronado.

from top, left to right
BAC Concorde
Britten-Norman BN-2 Islander
Boeing 747
Trident Two
McDonnell-Douglas DC-10
Lockheed Tri-Star
Boeing 727

Giants of the skies

The Dornier Do-X was in every sense a giant of the skies. When it first flew in July 1929 it was by far the largest aeroplane ever conceived. Even in the age of the Jumbo Jet its vast bulk would still command respect. Powered by twelve engines and spanning 48m, Do-X could lift 100 passengers plus a crew of ten.

In January 1931 the huge Dornier left Lisbon to cross the south Atlantic to Brazil. From there it flew north in easy stages to New York. The Do-X returned to Germany in 1932. On its journey it gave hundreds of thousands of people a glimpse of the future of air travel.

Even with the combined thrust of its twelve engines, the Do-X was still somewhat under-powered and on long ocean crossings the machine was sometimes flown very low over the surface of the water to benefit from the 'ground cushion' or 'surface' effect. This is a phenomenon that results from the build-up of pressure that can occur between an aeroplane structure and any relatively smooth surface. A machine flown in this way operates in air of much increased density. It becomes more efficient, requiring less power to support a given load and achieving greater range from a given quantity of fuel.

When the prototype Dornier Do-X was retired she was housed in a special museum in Berlin. Sadly both the museum and its giant exhibit were destroyed by Allied bombers.

Gigant was the name chosen for Messerschmitt's vast Me323 transport. Developed from the equally large Me321 troop and transport glider, it measured more than 54.9m from tip to tip. Power was provided by 6 Gnome Rhone radial engines, each delivering 1,140hp at take-off.

The Gigant was the biggest warplane used in the Second World War. It could carry up to 120 fully armed troops or twelve tons of freight, but its maximum speed was a mere 150mph (240km/h). Over the Mediterranean many of these lumbering giants fell to the guns of Allied fighters and bombers.

At the end of 1942 most of the Gigant squadrons were despatched from the Mediterranean to Russia to participate in the Stalingrad airlift. Vast quantities of food and ammunition were flown in to the beleaguered garrison and many wounded soldiers were flown out to hospitals in Germany. The Gigants were built largely by unskilled or semi-skilled workers. In all a total of 198 of these giant transports had been delivered to the Luftwaffe by the time production ceased in the spring of 1944.

Design of the Convair B-36 began in 1941 when the USAAF foresaw a need for a very long range bomber which could attack European targets from bases in America.

When B-36 entered service in 1948 it was the biggest and heaviest military aeroplane in the world. Spanning 64.6m, the huge bomber was powered by six 3,500hp engines driving pusher propellers. Later the power of these engines was increased to 3,800hp and a pair of 1,820kg thrust turbojets was hung under each wing tip. The combined power of those ten engines could push the B-36 through the air at 439mph (702km/h).

In 1953 a dozen B-36s were modified to carry Republic RF-84F Thunderflash fighters. These were intended for very long range high speed reconnaissance and strike missions. The RF-84Fs could be launched and retrieved by the B-36 mother ships in flight.

Dornier Do-X

Convair RB-36 with Republic RF-84F
about to hook on

Messerschmitt Me323 Gigant

D-1929

Warplanes that changed history

Twice in this century aircraft have decided the outcome of crucial battles which in turn decided the future course of history. Each time a seemingly unbeatable concentration of military power was defeated and scattered by an outnumbered defence. An example is the story of the Spitfire and Hurricane – and of the Battle of Britain which reached its climax on Sunday 15 September 1940....

In the late spring of 1940 Britain faced almost certain defeat. The German army, spearheaded by Stuka dive bombers and supported by 1,000 Messerschmitt Me109 fighters, had overrun France. Both the French and the British armies were routed. More than 300,000 soldiers were rescued from the beaches of Dunkirk, but their guns and fighting vehicles were left in the hands of the enemy.

The RAF also suffered heavy losses in the battle for France. More than 400 fighters – a quarter of its total strength – had been destroyed.

By 1 June the British stood alone and almost disarmed. A hushed House of Commons heard Winston Churchill announce '...the Battle of France is over...the Battle of Britain is about to begin!'

In southern England, German paratroops were expected at any moment and a strange arsenal of weapons was gathered to meet them. Antique pistols and muskets were commandeered from museums. Members of the Home Guard, lacking anything more deadly, were equipped with pikes and swords. Private cars were clad in iron sheets to serve in place of tanks.

The only effective fighting force was the RAF. Eight hundred Spitfires and Hurricanes now faced the combined might of three German *Luftflotten* ('air fleets') – the most powerful airforce the world had ever seen.

Fortunately for Britain the Luftwaffe had also suffered heavy losses. German aircrews were battle-weary and had to rest. For a month there was a lull as *Luftflotten* 2, 3 and 5 regrouped and reequipped. By 30 June 2,287 Luftwaffe aircraft stood ready for battle on airfields in Norway and along the Channel coast.

The RAF also made good use of the quiet spell. Men and machines were rested or replaced, and final adjustments were made to Fighter Command's elaborate system of ground-to-air control.

This control organization was the inspiration of Air Chief Marshal Sir Hugh Dowding, who had been appointed Commander-in-Chief of Fighter Command in 1936. At that time the RAF was equipped with biplane fighters – obsolete machines which were 100mph (160km/h) slower than bombers already in service with the Luftwaffe.

Hugh Dowding hastened development of the Spitfire and Hurricane. He also began construction of a chain of coastal radar stations. When the chain was complete, radar operators could plot hostile formations ninety miles (144km) away and estimate the number of aircraft, their course and their speed.

Behind the radar screen were the 'spotter' posts manned twenty-four hours a day by the men and women of the Observer Corps.

All information on aircraft approaching or overflying the British Isles was relayed to Dowding's HQ at Stanmore. From there it was relayed to Group headquarters and Sector Stations. From Sector Stations controllers spoke directly to fighter leaders in the air.

Battle began in the second week of July 1940. At first the Luftwaffe attacked convoys in the English Channel and many ships were sunk.

above *Supermarine Spitfire*
right *Hawker Hurricane*

The German plan was to lure British fighters over the Channel where they would be pounced on by high-flying Me109s. Then, when the Luftwaffe controlled the sky, the German army would roll across the Channel. The invasion, codenamed Operation Sealion, was already prepared. In French and Belgian ports thousands of barges waited to ferry tanks and troops over the narrow waters.

The plan failed because Dowding recognized the danger. He refused to commit large numbers of fighters to protect shipping. Even so, the RAF lost 145 fighters in July against the destruction of 270 Luftwaffe aircraft.

The loss of fighters, while serious, was not a crippling blow. By July, fighter production had risen to 200 planes a week, and such losses could be replaced.

The real problem, which was to plague Dowding throughout the battle, was the tragic loss of veteran fighter pilots. RAF Bomber and Coastal Commands, and the Navy's Fleet Air Arm, were combed for suitable flyers. Many other pilots came from occupied Europe, from the Dominions and from the USA.

Having failed to destroy the RAF over the Channel, Reichsmarshall Hermann Goering, Chief of the Luftwaffe, knew that time was running out. If England were to be invaded in 1940, Operation Sealion must begin before winter.

Goering decided that if the British would not come out and fight, his bombers must attack the RAF in its bases. August 13 was named as the day of the *Adlerangriffe* ('attacks of the eagles'). Goering boasted that in just four days the RAF would be destroyed.

'Eagle Day' began badly. Morning raids were cancelled because of fog. One formation of seventy-four Dornier 17s failed to hear the recall and began the battle alone, without fighters to protect them. Over Whitstable they were intercepted by Hurricanes which destroyed four and damaged others.

The afternoon of 'Eagle Day' saw savage attacks on airfields and installations. These attacks set the pattern for the weeks ahead when Fighter Command would be pounded unmercifully by day and by night.

But the Luftwaffe did not have things all its own way. On 15 August bombers of *Luftflotte* 5 left Norway on course for the north of England. German intelligence believed that Dowding had moved all his fighters to southern England. They expected the bombers of *Luftflotte* 5 to be unopposed.

They were wrong. Radar 'saw' the attackers far out to sea. Spitfire and Hurricane squadrons tore the German formations apart before they could even sight the English coast. As a result of heavy losses that day, *Luftflotte* 5 took no further part in the Battle of Britain.

Many reputations were to be shattered in that August of 1940. The dreaded Stuka had terrorized Europe from Warsaw to Dunkirk, but over the British coast Stuka squadrons were massacred by defending fighters and were quickly withdrawn from battle. Britain's Defiant, a two-seat fighter, proved no match for the Me109, and was relegated to night fighting.

The hardest blow for the Luftwaffe was the failure of the Me110. This twin-engined, long-range fighter, on which Goering had pinned such high hopes, was driven from the sky by British single-seaters.

But things were going badly for the RAF. By the last days of August Fighter Command was reeling from ferocious non-stop attacks. The shortage of fighter pilots became desperate. Men who had survived were exhausted by continuous battle and lack of sleep. Damage to control centres and telephone cables often cut all communication with fighter pilots in the air. It seemed that only a miracle could save the RAF from defeat.

The 'miracle' happened on the night of 24/25 August. Because of

faulty navigation, German bombers blasted civilian homes in east London. Hitler, who still hoped to make peace with Britain, had forbidden attacks against London. He was furious and ordered the bomber crews to be punished.

Winston Churchill then saw a chance to help Fighter Command. He ordered RAF Bomber Command to attack Berlin, knowing that this would enrage the German leader. Churchill was right. Hitler issued new orders to the Luftwaffe – London was to be bombed into submission.

As the Luftwaffe prepared for the assault, raids on Fighter Command bases slackened and ceased. Dowding could scarcely believe his luck. At the very moment when it seemed his Command might be destroyed, the unbearable pressure was eased. Fighter bases and control centres were speedily repaired, and weary pilots and ground crews enjoyed their first undisturbed sleep for many weeks.

The first all-out attack on London came on 7 September. It took the British by surprise. Many Luftwaffe formations were able to bomb their targets and return to base without ever sighting a British fighter. As the last bomber turned for home, London was ablaze. In Luftwaffe bases that night there was celebration. It was easy for German airmen to believe that RAF Fighter Command was finished.

Bad weather brought a lull. Then, at first light on 15 September, the airfields of *Luftflotten* 2 and 3 came to life. Soon British radar was tracking German reconnaissance flights. In control centres and airfields across southern England tension mounted. At 11.00 hours, plotters reported the build-up of massive formations over Calais and Boulogne. Fighter Command ordered all bases to instant readiness, and seventeen squadrons were scrambled to patrol the approaches to London.

Over the English coast RAF pilots saw an awe-inspiring spectacle. Vast formations of bombers and fighters stretched as far as the eye could see. A thousand warplanes were 'stacked' in layers from heights of 4,500 to 7,500 metres.

German pilots, who a few hours

Messerschmitt Me 109E being attacked by Supermarine Spitfire

before had celebrated the destruction of the RAF, now found Spitfires and Hurricanes attacking them from every side. All the way to London the fighting went on. As soon as one British squadron pulled out of the battle another took its place.

Over the target, battered Luftwaffe bombers were met head on by massed fighter squadrons which tore through their formations and made accurate bombing impossible.

Winston Churchill watched the progress of the battle at an RAF Group HQ at Uxbridge. As the fighting reached its peak he asked Air Vice-Marshal Park: 'What reserves do you have?' For a moment the Air Vice-Marshal was silent. Then he replied: 'There are none!' Every airworthy fighter had been committed – but it was enough. The Luftwaffe turned for home and were

harried all the way to the coast.

In the afternoon they came again, and again the fighters were waiting. The morning's battles were repeated, and still more burning wreckage marked the road to London. Sixty German aircraft had been destroyed. Many more were damaged beyond repair, limping home with burning engines and dying crewmen.

As evening mist obscured the wreckage of war, the Battle of Britain drew to its close. Within days Operation Sealion was abandoned. Britain remained free and southern England became the base for a mighty Anglo-American armada. In June 1944 that armada poured across the channel to liberate Western Europe.

Pilots scramble to their waiting Hurricanes

Battle for Midway

Douglas SBD-3 Dauntless

The Douglas SBD-3 Dauntless lacked the glamour of the Spitfire or the Hurricane. It was a naval dive bomber that had first seen service in 1938. By 1942 it was out of date. Faster, more heavily armed attack aircraft were already in service with the United States Navy. But at 10.24 on 4 June it was a formation of Dauntless bombers that was in position to strike the most devastating blow in naval history.

The story began on 2 December 1941. A Japanese carrier force under the command of Admiral Nagumo mounted a massive aerial strike on the US Pacific Fleet in its anchorage at Pearl Harbor in Hawaii.

The attack, made without declaration of war, was brilliantly planned and executed. Four American battle ships were sunk and four more were set ablaze. Great damage was inflicted on other ships and shore installations. In one most important respect, however, the attack was a failure. American aircraft carriers, prime targets for the Japanese bombers, were not at Pearl Harbor on that morning.

Admiral Yamamoto, Chief of the Imperial Japanese Navy, knew that if Japan were to win the Pacific war those carriers had to be destroyed. Although he commanded a fleet of the world's largest and most powerful battleships, Yamamoto believed that air power was the weapon of the future. He knew that the age of the giant battleship was over.

While the rest of Japan celebrated Pearl Harbor as a great victory,

Yamamoto began grimly to plan a new battle. This time American naval air power must be destroyed. He chose Midway Island as the target for a Japanese invasion. Midway, a tiny atoll 1,000 miles (1,600km) west of Pearl Harbor, was a vital US Navy outpost. Yamamoto knew that the Americans would defend it with their carrier force.

Meanwhile the Japanese went from victory to victory. Their power spread irresistibly across the Pacific and Indian oceans. Malaya, Borneo, Singapore, the Gilbert Islands, the Marianas and the Philippines all fell before the onslaught.

The British battleship *Prince of Wales* and the battle cruiser *Repulse* were sunk by shore-based bombers. A legend of invincible power began to grow around the Japanese.

The first set-back for the Imperial Navy came early in 1942. The battle of the Coral Sea was the first sea battle to be decided entirely by carrier-based bombers, with opposing surface vessels never coming within sight of each other. Losses in the Coral Sea were equal, with one carrier sunk and one damaged on each side. The result, however, was an American victory because the Japanese forces failed to capture their target – Port Moresby.

The Japanese believed that the American carrier damaged in the Coral Sea, the USS *Yorktown*, would be out of the war for many months. They did not think she would be able to interfere with their attack on Midway, which was now planned

for the beginning of June 1942.

They were wrong. *Yorktown* limped into Pearl on 27 May and, after almost super-human efforts by repair crews, she was declared battleworthy on 30 May. By 2 June *Yorktown* was sailing westward for Midway in company with the carriers *Hornet* and *Enterprise*. This carrier task force, escorted by cruisers and destroyers, was under the command of Admiral Fletcher.

US Navy intelligence units had cracked the Japanese battle codes. Admiral Nimitz, US Supreme Commander, therefore knew of Yamamoto's plans almost as soon as they were formulated. Nimitz, controlling his fleet from Pearl, prepared for the onslaught on Midway. He reinforced the island's ground and air defences and ordered Admiral Fletcher to bring the Japanese fleet to battle at the first opportunity.

Admiral Yamamoto, aboard the giant battleship *Yamato*, had sent submarines to picket Pearl Harbor and report US fleet movements. Unfortunately for the Japanese the subs did not reach their patrol lines until 3 June, by which time the American carriers were far to the west.

The vanguard of the Japanese fleet was the First Carrier Striking Force. It was under command of Admiral Nagumo, the admiral who had led the attack on Pearl, in the flagship carrier *Akagi*. The other carriers, all veterans of the Pearl attack, were *Kaga*, *Soryu* and *Hiryu*.

Nagumo sent out scout planes, but bad luck and faulty radio equipment prevented his pilots from spotting and reporting the American fleet. At midnight on 3 June Nagumo's ships were making maximum speed towards Midway, unaware that a powerful American carrier force was within a few hundred miles.

The Japanese carriers were escorted by the battleships *Harruna* and *Kirishima*, plus the heavy cruisers *Tone* and *Chikuma*. These powerful ships were backed up by a light cruiser and twelve destroyers. And that was only the spearhead. In the rear came the Imperial Battle Fleet of nine battleships, four aircraft carriers, eight heavy cruisers and a host of smaller vessels. More than 200 Japanese warships were now on course for Midway. Against this armada the Americans could muster just three aircraft carriers, eight cruisers, fifteen destroyers and twenty submarines. Small wonder, therefore, that Admiral Yamamoto was supremely confident of a decisive victory.

Battle was joined at first light on 4 June. At 04.54 Nagumo launched his first wave of bombers against Midway. At 05.30 a PBY Catalina flying boat reported the *Akagi* 150 miles (240km) north-west of Midway. Within minutes a second PBY spotted a large force of carrier bombers headed for the island.

Even as Midway's defences went to 'action stations', Nagumo's carriers were preparing to launch a second strike on the atoll. Almost all the remaining Japanese bombers were to be thrown into the attack. Only thirty-six torpedo planes, aboard *Akagi* and *Kaga*, were to be held back as a defence against American surface ships.

Before the second raid could be launched, the carriers were attacked by Avengers and Flying Fortresses from Midway. Although no damage was caused to the Japanese ships, the launching of the second Midway raid was delayed.

Nagumo now decided that the raid should be a maximum effort. He ordered deck crews to reload the thirty-six torpedo planes with bombs.

Yet again the launching of the second raid was delayed by

Midway-based bombers. Once more the Japanese ships escaped damage, but a nasty shock awaited Admiral Nagumo. A scout plane from the heavy cruiser *Tone* reported 'American carrier – believed *Yorktown!*'

At 08.30 bombers from the first Midway raid began returning to their carriers. Still the second wave of bombers waited to be launched.

At 09.00 Nagumo cancelled the second raid. He decided that *Yorktown* was his first concern and radioed Yamamoto that he was making all speed towards the American carrier. Then he reversed his order about the torpedo bombers. Sweating crews laboured on pitching decks to unload bombs and sling torpedos in their place. Discarded bombs were left in piles on the hangar decks. It was to be a fatal mistake!

At 09.18 the bombers were again ready for launch, this time against

Yorktown. Then a lookout spotted fifteen American Devastator torpedo bombers coming in at wave-top height. The carriers took evasive action. Zero fighters were launched and anti-aircraft guns blazed into action. The Devastators flew into an impenetrable wall of fire and steel. Every one was destroyed. The few torpedos that had been dropped were easily evaded by the Japanese ships.

The smoke and the din of battle had hardly died away when scout planes warned of more, and still more, formations of American naval bombers on the way. Nagumo knew now that there must be more than one enemy carrier nearby. But even as he ordered his ships to turn into wind and launch bombers, the lookout's warning was heard again. Two more waves of Devastators were boring in to attack.

Again the sky exploded into a fury of bursting shells and diving Zeros.

And yet again the carriers emerged unscathed. Forty-one Devastators from *Enterprise* and *Yorktown* had made the second attack. Six survived to return to their ships. Without fighter escort, the Devastator crewmen must have known that they had little chance of survival, but their sacrifice gave other Americans the chance to turn the tide of battle.

Anti-aircraft guns were still blazing at the scattered survivors when Nagumo again gave the order to turn into wind and launch bombers. But as the first machine hurtled down the flight deck of the *Akagi* the howl of its engine was joined by another sound. It was the anguished scream of a Japanese lookout.

Dropping like hawks from the sky came Dauntless dive bombers. Two bombs struck the *Akagi*, tearing a huge hole in the flight deck and destroying an aircraft lift. The great

ship might have survived, but piles of discarded bombs on the hangar deck now exploded in a monstrous chain reaction. Loaded bombers burst into flames adding to the inferno, and fuel stores ruptured sending blazing gasoline cascading through the vessel.

Sickened by the sight and smell of his dying flagship, Admiral Nagumo peered through the smoke and flame. His heart sank. To starboard the *Kaga* lay blazing from stem to stern. Further off he could see the ball of fire that was all that remained of the *Soryu*.

In the confusion of the earlier Devastator attacks *Hiryu* had become separated from her sister ships. Now she was the sole survivor. Her commander, Admiral Yamaguchi, now launched two strikes in quick succession against *Yorktown*. His pilots pressed home their attacks with desperate

gallantry, plunging through the hail of fire thrown up by *Yorktown* and her escorts. One pilot crashed his blazing bomber into the carrier's flightdeck. Three bombs and two torpedos ripped great holes in the doomed ship. At 14.45 hours *Yorktown* heeled over and the order was given to abandon ship.

As the surviving Japanese bombers turned towards *Hiryu* it seemed there might be a slim chance of snatching victory from defeat. The hope was short lived. At 17.00, as Yamaguchi was preparing to launch a further strike against the American fleet, the rising howl of a Dauntless motor heralded the last act of the drama.

One after another, forty dive bombers plummeted down on *Hiryu* and her consorts. White foaming wakes traced fantastic patterns across the blue-green water. The carrier twisted and turned in a desperate attempt to escape, but it was too late. Four bombs ripped her flight deck from end to end and newly re-armed bombers flamed and exploded.

As mighty *Hiryu* shuddered to a stop, what was possibly the greatest sea battle in history was ended, without opposing surface vessels ever sighting each other. In two brief actions lasting only a few minutes the Imperial Japanese Navy had lost its finest airmen, together with more than 300 bombers and fighters.

A long hard war had still to run its course in the Pacific, but from the evening of 4 June 1942 Japan was on the defensive, and the outcome of the war was never again in doubt.

At 10.42 hours on 4 June the first Dauntless from the USS *Enterprise* hurtled down upon the unsuspecting *Akagi* at the very moment that Admiral Nagumo's flagship began to launch her aircraft. Two bombs tore a gaping crater in the *Akagi*'s flight deck and started fires which soon raged throughout the length of the doomed ship. This was the turning point of the war in the Pacific. The Douglas SBD was said to have sunk more enemy combat tonnage than all other arms of the service combined.

Landmarks in airliner design

The first passenger aircraft were converted bombers left over from the 1914–18 war. Built of wood and canvas, they were noisy and uncomfortable. Often passengers sat in open cockpits exposed to wind and rain. But these flimsy machines were the first step on the road that led to the giant jetliners of today. On these pages we shall look at four aircraft which have revolutionized air travel.

The Junkers F.13 of 1919 was the first all-metal passenger aeroplane. Fitted with a 170hp engine, it had a cruising speed of 87mph (140km/h). Four passengers were carried in a comfortable enclosed cabin and each seat had a safety belt, now a standard fitting in all aircraft.

The wings, tail and fuselage of the F.13 were covered with corrugated Duralumin (a very strong alloy of aluminium). The aircraft could be fitted with wheels, floats or skis for operation from land, water or ice. It could be equipped to carry either passengers or cargo. A total of 322 Junkers F.13s were built and many continued in service until the Second World War.

The next big step in airliner design came in 1933 with the first flight of the Douglas Commercial DC-1. The DC-1 was a low-wing all-metal

aeroplane. The undercarriage was made retractable to reduce drag and increase speed. With twin 710hp engines the DC-1 carried fourteen passengers at a cruising speed of 178mph (284km/h).

Only one DC-1 was built, but Trans World Airlines (TWA) ordered forty copies of an improved version to be called DC-2. Other airlines hurried to order the new machine, and in October 1934 a DC-2 belonging to Royal Dutch Airlines (KLM) astounded the aviation world. Carrying a full load of passengers and mail it was placed second in the London to Melbourne air race.

An improved version of the DC-2 flew in 1935. Called DC-3, it could carry twenty-nine passengers at 195mph (312km/h). Many airlines ordered the DC-3 and large-scale production began at the Douglas factory in 1936.

Production continued until 1946. More than 11,000 were built, not counting the Li-2 version which was mass-produced by Soviet Russia. During the war the DC-3 flew with every major air force. In the United States it was called 'Skytrain' and in Britain it was named 'Dakota'. On and after D-Day 6 June 1944 (the day the Allies began the liberation of

The Junkers F.13 was the first all-metal passenger aircraft, seating four passengers

Europe) 'Dakotas' and 'Skytrains' carried tens of thousands of troops into battle. The DC-3 even served with the Luftwaffe, which used a captured machine on its wartime service to Portugal and Spain.

When the war ended, thousands of demobilized DC-3s provided a foundation for a new world-wide airline network. Today, more than forty years after the first flight, at least 500 DC-3s remain in airline service and the aircraft is a familiar sight at civil and military airfields around the world.

The 500mph (800km/h) de Havilland Comet first flew in England on 27 July 1949. With her swept-back wings and gleaming metal finish, she excited all who saw her in the skies over Hatfield and Farnborough.

More than 100mph (160km/h) faster than the fastest propeller-driven airliner, Comet carried thirty-six passengers in near-silent luxury. She flew over 12,000 metres high in the dark blue skies of the stratosphere, far above the storms and turbulence of the

The Douglas DC-3, known as Skytrain by the USAAF and Dakota by the RAF, carried thousands of allied soldiers in the Second World War

The de Havilland Comet, well over 160km/h faster than its fastest competitor, ushered in the age of the jetliner

lower atmosphere. The Comet went into service with British Overseas Airways Corporation. Soon everyone wanted to fly by jet. It was clear that propeller-driven airliners were out-of-date.

Then came a series of crashes which led to the suspension of all Comet services. The cause was metal fatigue (which causes metal to become brittle). The cure was relatively simple. All Comets were grounded and it was two years before new versions of the aircraft appeared on the world's air routes.

Today, although outdated by faster jetliners, Comets still give valuable service carrying 'package-tour' holidaymakers to the Mediterranean. And a new, more powerful version, named 'Nimrod' is in service with the RAF (see page 77).

Comet raised airliner speeds by 100mph (160km/h). Later, jetliners flew at more than 600mph (960km/h) but that was the limit that could be achieved with conventional aerodynamics and engines. The next step forward had to be through the 'sound barrier'.

The speed of sound (called 'Mach One' by scientists) was once thought to be the absolute limit for manned aircraft. Mach One is around 750mph (1,200km/h) at sea level, dropping to about 600mph (960km/h) in the upper atmosphere.

The first man to fly through the sound barrier was Captain Chuck Yeager in the rocket-powered Bell X-1. The date was 14 October 1947, and at that time supersonic flight was a hazardous undertaking. A British machine, the de Havilland 108, also 'went supersonic' in 1947, but it broke up, killing test pilot Geoffrey de Havilland. Gradually man learned to slip smoothly through the sound barrier, and soon military aircraft were flying at supersonic speed as a matter of routine.

In 1962 the British Aircraft Corporation and the French Sud-Aviation Company combined resources to build a supersonic airliner. Construction of two prototypes began in 1965. On 2 March 1969 Concorde 001 made her maiden flight from Toulouse, and 002 took off from Filton a month later. Concorde's cruising speed of 1,450mph (2,320km/h) halves the journey time between Europe and America. She represents the pinnacle of technological achievement, as in their day did F.13, the DC-3 and the Comet.

When Concorde entered service in January 1976 it was by far the most thoroughly tested airliner in aeronautical history. More than 5,000 hours of test flying by French- and British-assembled machines preceded the issues of the certificates of airworthiness. Then came a further 1,000 hours of testing on world airline routes. By comparison the total flight test time of the Boeing 747 was less than 1,000 hours.

The flight test programme, headed by chief test pilots Brian Trubshaw in Britain and André Turcat in France, had been remarkably trouble-free. The result of this unprecedented effort is a docile machine which, despite its jet fighter performance, can be flown by any competent jetliner captain after a minimum of familiarization training. Although it flies twelve miles high at well over twice the speed of any comparable airliner, Concorde fits easily into established airline patterns and procedures.

One day Concorde, too, will be outdated.

And already the designers of the McDonnell Douglas company are planning a hypersonic airliner, fuelled by hydrogen, to carry 500 passengers at a speed of 5,000mph (8,000km/h) on the very edge of space.

Airborne at Kittyhawk

At 10.35 Eastern Standard Time on Thursday 17 December 1903 man took a giant stride along the road of progress. On that cold, blustery morning Orville Wright lifted the Wright Flyer from its launching track at Kill Devil Hills near Kitty Hawk, North Carolina. His uncertain fluttering flight lasted for just twelve seconds and reached an airspeed of 35mph (56km/h). The Flyer climbed 3.7 metres above its launch point and covered a distance of 36.5 metres – little more than half the length of Concorde.

From that brief hop has come the worldwide aerospace industry we know today. Before Orville Wright died in 1948, man had flown faster than the speed of sound. Jet fighters had climbed eleven miles (17.6km) into the stratosphere. Giant

Orville and Wilbur Wright at the International Aviation Tournament, Long Island in 1910

hundred-seat airliners were spanning the Atlantic, and the V-2 rocket was already pointing the way to the mountains of the moon.

The Wright Flyer now occupies the place of honour in the Smithsonian Institute, Washington. In aviation history it marks the end of the first chapter. That chapter began with Sir George Cayley's model glider in 1804, and included such honoured names as Henson, Du Temple, Mozhaisky, Maxim, Ader, Langley, Pilcher and Lilienthal. They were men of many countries all inspired by the age-old dream of flight.

Some gave their lives in pursuit of that dream. Otto Lilienthal died in a gliding accident in 1896, and it was a report of his death that inspired the brothers Wilbur and Orville Wright to build their first model glider.

The Wrights owned a bicycle workshop in Dayton, Ohio. Both were skilled designers and engineers.

Their model had a span of 1.5 metres and was first flown as a kite in 1899. The experience it provided led to the construction of the first full-scale Wright glider in 1900.

Glider No.1 made its first few flights as a tethered kite. Later it was to give the brothers their first taste of free flight over the sand dunes of Kittyhawk. Glider No.2, launched in 1901, was less successful than its predecessor. Nevertheless it taught Wilbur and Orville vital lessons about aerodynamic control.

In 1902 the Wright brothers completed their third machine. Glider No.3 made more than 900 manned glides totalling nearly five hours in the air. The Wrights were now by far the most experienced pilots in the world. Glider No.3 was in all essentials an efficient flying machine. It lacked only a lightweight engine to achieve the goal of powered, sustained and controlled flight.

Since no suitable power plant was available, the Wrights set about designing an aero-engine of their own. When completed, it was a 3.3 litre 4-cylinder 4-stroke motor developing 13 brake-horse-power. Built into a new 3-metre-span airframe, it turned two 2.5-metre-diameter propellers by means of bicycle chains.

On Monday 14 December they were ready for the great adventure. Wilbur, the elder brother, won the toss of a coin and took the controls for the first take-off. The roar of the motor echoed over the dunes and the Flyer accelerated down the launching track. As the machine lifted, Wilbur pulled the nose up too steeply. The Flyer stalled and dropped heavily on the sand, smashing a spar. Repairs and bad weather delayed the next attempt until 10.35 on 17 December.

And then it was Orville's turn....

Specification of Wright Flyer No. 1
Span: 12.3m
Length: 6.43m
Wing chord: 1.97m
Wing area: 47.38m^2
Empty weight: 274kg
Loaded weight: approx. 340kg
Power plant: four-cylinder water-cooled engine developing 12bhp, driving two 2.59m diameter propellers by chains
Speed: 45km/h

Orville Wright takes off for his first flight in the Wright Flyer from sand dunes at Kill Devil Hills near Kitty Hawk

Gliding and soaring

Have you ever watched gliders soaring high in the sky and wondered how they manage to remain airborne for so long without an engine?

A glider is always descending relative to the air around it. Lacking an engine, the glider pilot utilizes the force of gravity to draw him forward and downward. In other respects the glider is subject to the same forces of lift, weight and drag as a powered aircraft.

Imagine a glider which sinks at a rate of 1 metre every second. Now think of that machine gliding 'downhill' through a large bubble of still air. Compared with the air in the bubble the glider loses height at 1 metre per second. If, however, the bubble itself is rising at 3 metres per second relative to the outside air, the glider will in fact be climbing at $(3-1)$ 2 metres per second. Equally, if the bubble should descend at 3 metres per second, relative to surrounding air, the glider will descend at $(3+1)$ 4 metres per second.

Such bubbles of air do in fact exist, and when they are rising we call them thermal. Air on the hilltops has gas rising from a factory chimney. It may be air which has been heated by contact with a hot tarmac road or runway. Or it may be air that has been trapped and heated in a field of ripening corn.

Most thermals occur while the sun is well above the horizon. Occasionally, on a cool calm evening, a pilot will be surprised to find a thermal rising strongly from a fold in the hills. This is an 'adiabatic' thermal. Air on the hilltops has cooled and poured down the hillside, displacing the warmer air in the valley.

A glider pilot cannot see hot air rising, although it is sometimes possible to see its effects. Birds are great soaring enthusiasts, and thermals are often indicated by them, as they lazily circle on outstretched wings. The most important pointer to thermal activity, however, is the cumulus cloud.

Warm air can hold more invisible water vapour than cold air. If that warm air begins to rise it loses heat at the rate of 3°F per 305m. As it cools a point is reached when the water vapour condenses into cloud.

On a warm sunny day thermals are marked by fluffy white cumulus cloud. While a cumulus is still forming and growing, a pilot can be sure of finding an upcurrent under the leading edge of the cloud. He must always remember that where there are upcurrents there are also downcurrents. These often occur under the downwind edge of the cloud.

Sometimes long 'streets' of cumulus will occur and then it is possible to travel long distances, climbing under one cloud and then gliding to the next. Sometimes a cumulus will appear, grow for a little while, and then decay and disappear. At other times the little fluffy cloud will grow until it becomes a monster. Then it is called Cumulonimbus or CuNim for short. This is thunderstorm cloud with a leaden grey base and pearly white tops rising 13,500m into the air.

Glider pilots approach such clouds with caution and enter them at their peril. Below the cloud, powerful upcurrents reach 7.6m per second and more. Inside, the turbulence is often sufficient to tear a glider apart. Every few minutes a pilot will be blinded by lightning and deafened by thunder. Torrential rain lashes down almost incessantly, sometimes giving way to hailstones which pound the glider like drumsticks beating a big drum.

Glider pilots are not entirely dependent upon thermals for soaring flight. When a wind blows at right angles to a long hillside, the air is forced upwards. The stronger the wind, the greater the upcurrent. If you visit a hillside gliding site like Dunstable or Kirbymoorside you will see gliders flying elongated figures of eight. They beat along the hillside, turn into wind and then beat back the way they have come. In this way even

a relatively inexperienced pilot can remain airborne for long periods.

A glider is controlled in the same way as a power aircraft. The control column operates the ailerons and elevator while the rudder is worked by foot pedals. Instrumentation is simple, consisting of Air Speed Indicator (ASI), altimeter, turn and bank indicator and a variometer. The variometer indicates the rate of rise or sink in feet or metres per second. If a pilot is attempting an altitude flight he will also have a baragraph. This instrument gives a permanent record of the flight in terms of altitude and duration.

At the start of a flight a glider must be towed into the air. The usual method is by winch tow. The winch has a drum driven by a powerful motor. A long steel cable is attached to the nose of the glider. The winch driver then begins to wind the cable onto the drum, pulling the glider up into the air. In good conditions a skilled pilot can reach a height of almost 500m. The other method is by aero-tow. Here the glider is joined to a light aircraft by a 45.75m rope. Aero-towing is more expensive than winching, but it gives the pilot greater altitude to begin his flight.

top left *Skylark 4*
top right *Kestrel 17 and tug*
bottom *BS-1 glider (designed by Bjorn Stender) with Auster tug*
far right *Kestrel 19*

Aircraft at work

Drought and forest fire; man's oldest enemies go hand in hand. The sun beats down on moisture-starved trees. Fallen branches litter the ground. The undergrowth dies and dries. The forest becomes a giant bonfire waiting for the spark that will set it ablaze.

It begins with a wisp of smoke drifting up through tinder-dry trees. Then an entire hillside explodes into flame. Animals and birds flee in panic. Trees burst apart and flames roar some eighty feet (24m) into the air. It may have been a carelessly discarded cigarette, a picnic fire allowed to smoulder on, or the sun's rays concentrated through a broken bottle. The cause no longer matters. The fire is spreading with every second, and lives are in danger.

That first wisp of smoke was seen by a forest ranger high up in his watchtower. A radio message has alerted the firefighters, the dedicated men who will fight the blaze with picks, shovels, axes, and even dynamite. Parachute commandos are standing by to make a perilous drop into the seat of the fire. And this time a new weapon will be used....

There is a snarl of powerful motors. Low over the tree tops a big yellow flying boat lines up for a run over the heart of the blaze. As the fingers of flame reach up towards the red and yellow hull a great white cascade bursts from the underside. Seven tons of water crash down among the burning trees. Huge branches are torn down and trunks are scattered like matchsticks. As the deluge hits the ground it is flung up into the trees again to descend as a man-made rainstorm over acres of trees as yet unburned.

Enveloped in steam and smoke, the water bomber turns away. This is the Canadair CL-215. Over the nearest stretch of open water she will descend to skim the surface and scoop up another bomb load. Then within minutes she will head back for the fire. The CL-215 is a two-motor amphibian flying boat. When not employed as an aerial fire engine it can carry passengers or cargo to remote areas, landing on any short stretch of open water.

The idea of aeroplanes working in the service of man goes back to the years before the First World War. An airmail service began in India in 1911. In Britain, letters and newspapers were carried from Hendon to Windsor to celebrate the coronation of King George V. In those early days, however, aircraft were frail structures with little power to spare to carry anything other than pilot and fuel.

Four years of war changed the picture completely. Aero engines increased in power by 400 per cent. Tough two-seat biplane bombers such as the de Havilland DH-4 and DH-9 had been built in thousands. When peace returned these fine aeroplanes were to prove willing aerial workhorses.

In May 1918 the US Post Office inaugurated an airmail service between Washington and New York. The pilots of the US Mail flew their DH-4s with the same courage that had characterized the riders of the Pony Express in the previous century. The mail went out in all weathers by day and by night. Flying instruments were primitive. Night-flying aids consisted of bonfires lit on high hills along the route. Planes crashed and pilots died, but mostly the mails got through.

The exploits of the mail pilots caught the imagination of the American people. Their success encouraged the development of blind-flying instruments and purpose-designed mailplanes. Gradually a countrywide network of mail routes was built up, and with the development of reliable passenger airliners that network became the basis for the vast transcontinental airline network that today serves every part of the USA.

Another less serious job for de-mobilized fighting planes was entertaining the public. It was called 'barnstorming'. One or two garishly painted biplanes would arrive in a meadow on the outskirts of town. Bills would be posted advertising fantastic feats of airmanship. Next day the fun would begin: aerobatics with trails of coloured smoke, joy-rides at a dollar a trip. Chivalrous

pilots would pick up a lady's handkerchief with a wingtip. A daring young lady would walk on a wing in flight, or swing from the undercarriage on a trapeze.

One barnstorming pilot picked up fuel from a moving lorry. Another went one better and refuelled from another aircraft air-to-air. It was all good fun guaranteed to make the crowd rock with laughter or gasp with surprise.

Some of the stunts lived on. First the USAAF and then pioneer Alan Cobham developed flight refuelling. Today the one-time circus stunt has become a vital routine operation in every major air force.

An extension of barnstorming was the art of aerial advertising. An unknown pilot at an air show used his smoke trail generator to write a brief message across the sky. A local tradesman saw the possibilities, and skywriting was born. For many years it was practised on both sides of the Atlantic.

Other advertisers used towed banners to publicize their products. Leaflets were scattered over towns and cities. Aircraft were fitted with powerful loud-hailers, and slogans were shouted above the roar of the engine.

Most methods of aerial advertising have been banned because they cause a public nuisance. Skyshouting lives on as police procedure for controlling crowds, while opposing factions in civil wars occasionally stop shooting at each other to scatter propaganda leaflets instead.

By the 30s aeroplanes had proved their reliability and load carrying capability. Aircraft could not yet compete with surface transport in terms of economy, but the aerial freighter was fast and it could land in places that surface vehicles could not reach.

It was the ability to go anywhere that led to the continuing saga of the 'bush pilot'. There were, and still are, large areas of the earth's surface where roads are either very poor or non-existent – where there are no railways or established airfields. These are the territories where the bush pilot flourishes.

Australia, New Guinea, Alaska, Canada, Africa and South America all have large 'backwoods' areas where civilization depends almost entirely upon aviation. A bush pilot can find somewhere to land and take off in the most forbidding territory: a lake or a river; a stretch of level sand; hard packed snow or a

stretch of glacier. With wheel, ski or float – and with an iron nerve – the bush pilot will get in and out with his precious load of food, medicine or drilling equipment.

The Noorduyn Norseman is typical of the workplanes designed for operation in outback territories. Capable of operating from land or water, ice or snow, the Norseman first saw service among the rugged mountains and forests of North America. During the War it served with the USAAF.

Bush pilots have opened up the wilderness. Prospectors have found riches almost beyond belief, such as iron, gold, plutonium, silver, aluminium, coal and oil, in areas once considered worthless. After the prospectors came the mining engineers and the oilmen. Now the demand is for bigger aeroplanes with short take-off and landing (STOL) performance to carry mining equipment, generators, drilling rigs, tractors and living accommodation. Today there is a new generation of backwoods aeroplanes: Islander, Skyvan, Nomad, Twin Otter and Skyservant.

In 1911 a Presbyterian missioner, the Reverend John Flynn, arrived in central Australia. His mission was to

Canadair CL-215 acts as an aerial fire engine and discharges its bomb load of water over the burning trees

aid and comfort the people of the tiny settlements scattered over thousands of miles of bushland. He saw people suffer and die for lack of medical aid. There seemed no way in which he could help. Then, in 1917, he had a dream. He saw how the fledgling aeroplane and the newly invented wireless telephony could be combined to bring aid to the remotest family.

To most people his ideas seemed to belong to the realms of science fantasy, but he began to campaign, and gradually he won allies. Money was donated. By 1926 doctors and aircraft were available, but a reliable transmitter-receiver was needed to bring help speedily to isolated homesteads.

Wireless engineer Alfred Traeger solved the problem with a pedal operated set which transmitted and received morse code. In 1929 the 'Aerial Medical Services of Australia' was established at Cloncurry Base. To the public it was 'the Flying Doctor' from the start, and in 1942 the name was changed to the Flying Doctor Service.

The service grew to cover the

top *Noorduyn Norseman, a backwoods plane*
below *Beagles of the Royal Flying Doctor Service at Broken Hill, New South Wales*

whole of central Australia. The pedal generated W/T set gave way to battery powered R/T (radio-transmitter) – clear speech instead of morse code. After a quarter of a century there were a thousand sets and ten airbases. When not in use for matters of life or death, the R/T could be used for social contact with a next door neighbour a hundred miles away. Children could attend the 'School of the Air' in which teachers and pupils may be scattered over half a continent.

The Reverend John Flynn, in the words of his mission, spread a mantle of safety over the great empty spaces of Australia. His monument is a pre-historic granite monolith on which are carved the words 'He brought gladness and rejoicing to the wilderness and solitary places'. Today John Flynn's mantle of safety has covered New Guinea, and is spreading across the continent of Africa.

Aircraft are also helping to feed the world's ever growing population. Fishery research aircraft like the long-range Islander spot and track shoals of fish. In addition to steering the trawler fleets to the most promising fishing grounds, they can provide an overall picture of the sea's resources.

Over land, aircraft control locusts and other insect pests by spraying breeding grounds with insecticides. They are also employed to spread chemical fertilizers over crops and grazing land.

'Crop dusting' requires a special type of pilot. The work is dirty and dangerous. The aircraft must be flown with great accuracy along equally spaced tracks. It must keep close to the ground to deposit the dust or spray evenly and prevent it from spreading to other crops. A weed killer intended for a field of young corn would kill cabbages or fruit trees in the next field.

Flying low is hazardous. At the end of each run the pilot has to make a steep 180° turn to commence his next run as soon as possible. He may also have to avoid trees or power lines, and when his hopper is empty he must land, reload and take off again in the very shortest possible time.

Cessna Agwagon. This specialized agricultural aeroplane was designed specifically for spraying and dusting crops, sowing seeds and distributing fertilizer

Test Pilot

'Test Pilot' conjures up an image of a daring young man in a leather flying jacket doing crazy aerobatics, or diving at incredible speed to pull out a few inches above the grass.

That's how it is in the Hollywood film fantasies. In real life the test pilot is more likely to be a cautious, dedicated man with many years of flying to his credit. Often he will also be a highly qualified scientist, able to combine practical flying with the most advanced aerodynamic theory.

The test pilot's job combines long periods of routine trials with moments of danger and excitement. Above all, the purpose of test flying is to make an aeroplane safe for other aircrew to fly.

Some aircraft are 'rogues' from the very beginning. During the Second World War there was a torpedo bomber named Botha. It had a reputation for going out of control when its warload was released. The machine was extensively tested by the Government flight test centre at Boscombe Down. The official report on the Botha ended with the words: 'Entry into this aircraft is difficult – it *should* be made impossible!'

The Botha was a 'bad-un' with few redeeming features. Another wartime aircraft, the Typhoon, also got off to a very bad start. The fact that the Typhoon became a decisive war-winning weapon is a tribute to the civilian and service test pilots who ironed out the 'bugs'.

The Hawker Typhoon was designed to replace the Hurricane. With four 20mm cannon and a top speed of 420mph (672km/h), it should have been a match for any Luftwaffe fighter. When war began in

top *the experimental jet-powered Short SC-1 was the world's first successful vertical take-off aeroplane*

above *Edward Heath in the cockpit of Concorde with Brian Trubshaw, chief test pilot of BAC*

September 1939, the first Typhoon was nearing completion. Its first flight took place in February 1940. Development was slow. There were problems with both the airframe and the brand new Napier Sabre engine. By the end of 1940 the RAF desperately needed a new fighter to combat the Focke-Wulf FW 190.

Because of this, the Typhoon was thrown into the battle before all its problems had been solved.

The result was a near disaster. Of the first 142 delivered to Fighter Command, 135 were damaged or destroyed in accidents. Engines would burst into flames without warning. Structural failures occurred

BAC TSR2

Hawker Typhoon

during manoeuvres at high speed. At one stage it seemed certain that the Typhoon would be scrapped.

Fortunately the test pilots were given time to identify and solve the problems. In 1943 the Hawker Typhoon began to show its true value in combat with low-flying Focke-Wulf FW 190 fighter bombers. But the Typhoon's moment of destiny was still to come.

In 1944 Typhoon squadrons began flying offensive sweeps over France. Armed with bombs and rockets in addition to cannon, they destroyed German road and rail communications. Other targets included V-1 and V-2 launching sites.

The Typhoon's rocket projectile was both simple and deadly. A length of iron pipe 76.2mm in diameter and tipped with a 27kg warhead, it could destroy a steam locomotive or a Tiger Tank with a single hit.

When the Anglo-American armies smashed into Normandy in June 1944, the lightly armed and armoured Allied tanks proved no match for the German Tigers and King Tigers. The weapon which saved the day was the *Tyffy-bomber*. Squadrons of rocket-firing Typhoons patrolled at a height of 3,000 metres over the battle area. Operating a 'cab-rank' system, the pilots waited to be called down on

specific targets by RAF liaison officers riding in the leading tanks.

During the crucial battle of the Falaise Gap, Typhoons tore the German panzer divisions to shreds. Enemy armoured columns would be halted by the destruction of the leading vehicles. Then the rest would be picked off one by one. Many tank commanders surrendered or abandoned their machines in the face of such a fierce onslaught. The Typhoon thus played a vital part in the battle for Normandy, and proved to be a weapon that was saved from the scrapheap by the dedicated work of the test pilot.

Unlike the Typhoon, some aircraft are right from the very first flight. The Mosquito was an example of a warplane that needed little modification before it was brought into service. Another machine which, despite its complexity, caused few problems for its test pilots, was the TSR2. TSR2 (Tactical Strike Reconnaissance) was designed to

replace the RAF's ageing Canberra and Vulcan bombers. Operating from short unprepared airstrips, it could carry approximately 4,550kg of air-to-ground missiles over very long ranges at twice the speed of sound. 'Terrain clearance' radar allowed it to approach its target 'on the deck', automatically guiding the aircraft through valleys and over hills. TSR2 made her first flight on 27 September 1964. The pilot was Wing Commander R. P. Beaumont, one of the service pilots who played a vital part in the Typhoon story.

Test flying proceeded smoothly. There were no serious problems. It seemed that the new bomber was set for an early introduction into service. TSR2 was certainly the most advanced weapon system in the world. With it, the RAF would have had an advantage over any possible adversary. Sadly, the TSR2 had political enemies who exaggerated its cost. Following a change of government, the TSR2 programme was cancelled and the American F-111 ordered in its place.

It was a poor bargain, for F-111, unlike TSR2, was plagued with problems from the start. Many of them crashed, and major components had to be completely redesigned. Soon it became clear that the F-111 would be both expensive and unreliable. It, too, was cancelled at considerable cost.

Then a new Anglo-French design – the AFVG – was ordered 'off the drawing board'. Millions of pounds were spent on research, only for the AFVG to be cancelled in its turn. TSR2 could have been in full squadron service by 1970. Instead, twelve years after that brilliant first flight, RAF pilots are still equipped with obsolete Canberras and Vulcans.

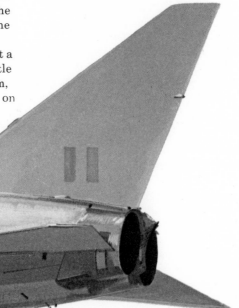

XR219

Wooden wonders

The de Havilland DH 91 Albatross was a remarkable aeroplane. When it first flew in May 1937, it was without question the most beautiful airliner of them all. A low-wing monoplane, with twin fins and rudders, it was powered by four closely cowled Gypsy Twelve engines.

The fuselage was of almost perfectly streamlined form, its circular cross section fairing gracefully into a smoothly tapering wing. But the really remarkable fact about this 32-metre-span airliner was that it was constructed entirely of wood.

The fuselage shell was a sandwich of two layers of plywood filled with a balsa-wood core. The whole structure was moulded in one piece on a collapsable jig. Door and window apertures were sawn into the completed structure after the jig had been removed. The wing was built in one piece from spruce, plywood and balsa. The tail unit was similarly constructed, and all external surfaces were coated in a special cotton fabric.

Albatross could carry twenty-two passengers at a cruising speed of 220mph (352km/h). It was a popular machine with its crews and, in the hands of an experienced pilot, this big aeroplane was almost as manoeuvrable as a fighter.

Five aircraft were completed and delivered to Imperial Airways, the forerunner of the British Overseas Airways Corporation, now known as British Airways. Two more were requisitioned by the Air Ministry for service with the transport squadrons of the RAF. By then it was the summer of 1939. It was clear that a world war was inevitable, and development of this very promising airliner came to an end. Soon the five civilian machines joined their sister ships in the RAF. One suffered a crash landing and the others were written-off one by one in minor accidents.

By the middle of 1943 the graceful Albatross had vanished from the skies. Had war not intervened, she might well have played a significant role in the history of air transport. One can imagine, for example, a Super Albatross powered by four Merlin engines and carrying eighty passengers at 300mph (480km/h).

Although the Albatross did not achieve the full promise of her early days, the lessons learned from the unique method of construction led directly to another more famous de Havilland aeroplane – the Mosquito. The prototype of the Mosquito flew for the first time on 25 November 1940. Like the Albatross it was constructed of plywood, spruce and balsa. In outline it was reminiscent of a still earlier wooden aeroplane, the famous de Havilland Comet racer of 1934. Right from its very first flight the bright yellow prototype, unfairly christened 'Yellow Peril',

demonstrated a performance that, by the standards of the time, was truly staggering.

Mosquito was designed as an unarmed high-speed bomber. Powered by two Merlin engines, it had a maximum speed of 380mph (608km/h) – 40mph (64km/h) faster than the Spitfire. It could carry a bomb load of up to 8,800kg – equal to the payload of a four-motor Stirling heavy bomber.

The de Havilland designers promised even more. New, more powerful Merlins would boost the speed to more than 420mph (672km/h). This was faster than the fastest fighter in service anywhere in the world. Plans were prepared to build Mosquitoes tailored for a multitude of military duties. As production increased the new machine went into action. First as a bomber, then as night fighter,

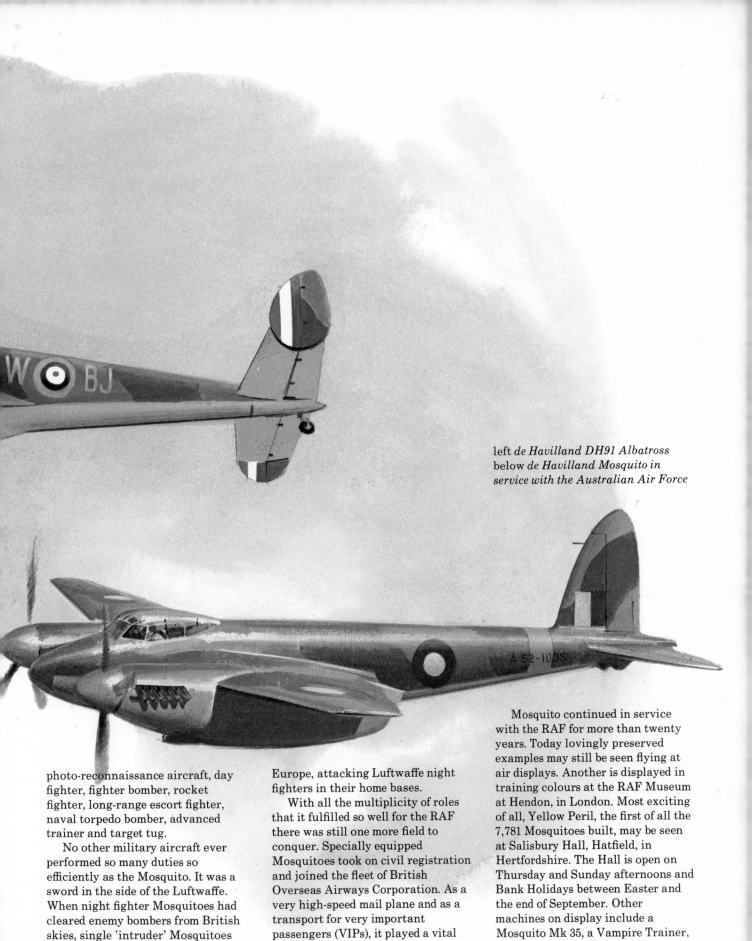

left *de Havilland DH91 Albatross*
below *de Havilland Mosquito in
service with the Australian Air Force*

photo-reconnaissance aircraft, day
fighter, fighter bomber, rocket
fighter, long-range escort fighter,
naval torpedo bomber, advanced
trainer and target tug.

No other military aircraft ever
performed so many duties so
efficiently as the Mosquito. It was a
sword in the side of the Luftwaffe.
When night fighter Mosquitoes had
cleared enemy bombers from British
skies, single 'intruder' Mosquitoes
took to roaming the night skies of

Europe, attacking Luftwaffe night
fighters in their home bases.

With all the multiplicity of roles
that it fulfilled so well for the RAF
there was still one more field to
conquer. Specially equipped
Mosquitoes took on civil registration
and joined the fleet of British
Overseas Airways Corporation. As a
very high-speed mail plane and as a
transport for very important
passengers (VIPs), it played a vital
part in the secret diplomacy of war.

Mosquito continued in service
with the RAF for more than twenty
years. Today lovingly preserved
examples may still be seen flying at
air displays. Another is displayed in
training colours at the RAF Museum
at Hendon, in London. Most exciting
of all, Yellow Peril, the first of all the
7,781 Mosquitoes built, may be seen
at Salisbury Hall, Hatfield, in
Hertfordshire. The Hall is open on
Thursday and Sunday afternoons and
Bank Holidays between Easter and
the end of September. Other
machines on display include a
Mosquito Mk 35, a Vampire Trainer,
and a Venom NF3.

41

Spy in the sky

Aerial surveillance probably began with tethered hydrogen balloons during the Franco-Prussian war of 1870. Then aircraft came on the scene. In the First World War, Fighting Scouts such as the SE5A ranged over enemy lines reporting artillery positions and troop concentrations.

Between 1918 and 1939 aerial reconnaissance continued in secrecy. Germany used the gigantic *Graf Zeppelin* airship for the secret observation of newly constructed British radar stations. The British, meanwhile, employed a seemingly innocent Lockheed 12A, lavishly equipped with German Leica cameras, to photograph large areas of the Third Reich.

When the Second World War began, aerial reconnaissance was developed to a fine art. High altitude versions of fighter and bomber aircraft probed enemy defences. Targets were photographed before bombing attacks and again, afterwards, to assess the damage caused. Aerial reconnaissance over the secret German experimental

Lockheed SR-71A, a strategic reconnaissance aircraft in the service of the United States Air Force

Lockheed U-2, long-range, high altitude aircraft

establishment at Peenemünde revealed the V-1 and V-2 secret weapons and gave the Allies time to prepare a defence.

After the war ended, countries who had been allies during the war became further and further estranged. One result of this was that Britain and the United States carried out photographic reconnaissance around and sometimes over Russian and Chinese territories. At the same time Russian spy machines overflew western Europe and probed the coasts of the United States.

New surveillance techniques were perfected. 'Sideways looking' radar could scan an area forty-five miles (72km) wide on either side of a search plane. Delicate electro-magnetic equipment could detect variations in the earth's magnetic field and pin-point a nuclear submarine 300 metres below the surface of the ocean.

These activities received little publicity until 1 May 1960. On that day an American pilot named Gary Powers had the misfortune to earn himself a novel place in history. A Russian guided missile destroyed his aircraft over Sverdlovsk in the USSR. Powers was captured, tried as a spy and imprisoned. That caused an international sensation. Even more sensational was the aeroplane he was flying. Known as U-2, it had been designed and built by the Lockheed company for long-range, very high-altitude reconnaissance.

U-2 was a massive 2.4-metre-span sailplane fitted with a single powerful jet engine. It could cruise at 500mph (800km/h) and climb to over 21,000 metres. Then, with the engine off, it could glide silently for hundreds of kilometres.

U-2 continues in service today, but it has been superseded by a still more advanced machine. This is the Lockheed A-11, otherwise known as the SR-71A strategic reconnaissance aircraft. SR-71A is a machine straight out of science fiction. A 30.5-metre-long black-painted monster, it can fly at more than 2,300mph (3,680km/h) on the very edge of space. It carries the most advanced electronic surveillance equipment ever designed. Its cameras produce extremely fine detail, and infra-red sensors record even the warm spot on a concrete runway from which a jet has taken off.

Above even the 27,400-metre cruising height of the SR-71A are the reconnaissance satellites, orbiting in the silence of space. These untiring automatic eyes cross and re-cross every square mile of the earth's surface. Nothing escapes them. Every rocket silo, every tank regiment, every aircraft carrier and every bomber base is faithfully recorded and reported.

To complete our story of aerial reconnaissance we must go almost from the sublime to the ridiculous. During the Vietnam war, the US Air Force needed to pinpoint enemy troops and vehicles hiding in dense jungle. Lockheed again provided the answer – Q-Star – a small powered sailplane with a silenced engine and propeller. Painted in non-reflective black finish, the two-seater Q-Stars flew night patrol over the jungles and mountains of Vietnam.

At a distance of about 150 metres the aircraft made a noise like the rustle of leaves. From the ground it could not be detected, but from the observer's seat in Q-Star a great deal could be 'seen'. Infra-red sensors could detect the warm engine of a parked vehicle at a range of more than 900 metres, and a super-sensitive 'people-sniffer' could locate an enemy soldier purely by his scent.

The Vietnam war is over for Q-Star, but back home in America it still searches in the night sky. Now, however, the pilot is a game warden and the target is a poacher raiding wildlife in the Florida Everglades.

Lockheed Q-Star, with engine muffling and long wingspread, developed from a Schweizer SGS 2-32 sail plane

Aeronautical museums

The skies over Hendon in north London once echoed to the roar of aero engines and the cheers of an excited crowd. Before the Second World War Hendon airfield was famous for its aerial pageants.

Hawker Harts and Fairey Hendons would bomb cardboard targets with vivid flashes and thunderous bangs. Gleaming Gloster Gauntlets would perform aerobatics, their wings tied together with ribbons; a Mark 1 Hurricane would astonish the crowd with its incredible speed of 320mph (512km/h).

That was all a very long time ago. Now the skies of Hendon are more likely to echo to the rumble of a Jumbo jet on its final approach to Heathrow. But below, in the famous Hendon hangars, history lives on.

Those hangars have been transformed into a magnificent modern museum. Outside, towering over everything, stands a huge Blackburn Beverley transport aircraft. Inside is a unique collection of the aircraft that have served with the RAF since its earliest days.

Exhibits range from a Bleriot XI of 1914 to the 1,500mph (2,400km/h) English Electric P-1B Lightning. The famous fighters of the First World War – SE5A, Gunbus, Camel, Pup and Triplane – are there. So, too, are the Spitfire, Hurricane, Defiant, Beaufighter, Typhoon and Tempest of the Second World War.

Bombers include a replica of the Vickers Vimy and the famous Lancaster 'S for Sugar' which survived 125 missions over Europe. Other famous aeroplanes include the Lysander, Wellington, Stranraer flying boat, Meteor and Canberra.

One especially interesting exhibit is the Gloster Gladiator display. The Gladiator was the last biplane fighter to serve with the RAF. In the museum stands aircraft No. 40468, resplendent in silver finish with the insignia of No. 87 Squadron. Nearby are the remains of Gladiator N5628 of No. 263 Squadron.

In April 1940, 263 Squadron was operating from the ice of Lake Lesjaskog in Norway. The Luftwaffe bombed the ice and many Gladiators sank in the frozen water. N5628 lay on the bed of the lake for thirty years. Today she can be seen just as she was, having been lifted from the lake by an RAF salvage crew in 1970.

Other historic aircraft may be seen at the Imperial War Museum and at the Science Museum in London.

The Science Museum houses many of the aeroplanes described in this book. There is Cayley's 1804 model glider, a Lilienthal 'hang' glider and a replica of the Wright Flyer. The Supermarine S-6B is there. So are the Hurricane and Spitfire, a Messerschmitt Me163 rocket fighter, a V-1 flying bomb and many others. There is also a magnificent collection of aircraft models that traces the development of aviation in the twentieth century.

Across the channel at Meudon, near Paris, is the famous Musée de l'Air. Here can be seen one of the most exciting collections of historic aircraft in the world. Under one roof is housed an incredible variety of flying machines dating back to the earliest years of French aviation. Warplanes preserved there include a Spad, a Pfalz D XII, a Fokker D VII, a Nieuport Scout and a de Havilland DH9 from the First World War. From the Second World War there are a Dewoitine D 520, a Morane-Saulnier MS 406, a Focke-Wulfe 190, a Spitfire, a Heinkel 162 Volksjäger, and a Russian Yak-9.

The museum also has on display famous machines from French history, such as the dainty Antoinette and the long-range Point d'Interrogation ('question mark') which in 1929 crossed the Atlantic from Paris to New York. And in sharp contrast there are the science fiction shapes of the first French supersonic aeroplanes: the Leduc O.10 Ramjet and the Trident rocket/jet.

below *French long-range Point d'Interrogation*
bottom *Gunbus fighter*

Museum in the sky

A small grass airfield on a sunny afternoon: white clouds sail briskly across the deep blue sky. A bright yellow windsock streams from its pole. Colourful biplanes line up waiting their turn to fly. Then there is the snarl of a powerful motor. Excited children point to the sky as a Bristol Fighter roars past.

You might think that this is a scene from a flying display in the 20s.

You would be wrong. This is Old Warden Aerodrome and the time is now. Most of the aeroplanes belong to the Shuttleworth Trust. Others are privately owned and have flown in specially for the display.

below: *de Havilland Comet Racer which won the London–Melbourne race*; centre: *Stearman Cadet*; bottom: *SE5A*

The Shuttleworth Collection of historic aircraft is based at Old Warden aerodrome near Biggleswade in Bedfordshire. It is a living museum. As many of the exhibits as possible are maintained in flying condition and may be seen in their natural element. Pageants and special flying days are organized throughout the summer season. At other times both flying and non-flying exhibits may be viewed under cover in the hangars. Visitors are welcome any day, except at Christmas.

Airworthy machines which can be seen at Old Warden include: Avro 504K, Avro Tutor, Blackburn Monoplane (the oldest British aircraft still flying), Bristol F2B, Deperdussin, Gloster Gladiator, LVG (German WW1), SE5A, Percival Provost, Sopwith Pup and others.

In addition to preserving existing vintage aircraft, the Shuttleworth Trust devotes great efforts to seeking out derelict machines and then restoring them, where possible, to flying condition. An exciting example is the LVG, a colourful German two-seater from the First World War which now excites crowds at air displays all over England.

One of the Trust's most ambitious projects concerns the de Havilland Comet Racer. Registered G-ACSS and named *Grosvenor House*, this machine has been called 'the most historic famous aircraft in existence'

In October 1934, C. W. A. Scott and T. Campbell Black flew G-ACSS to victory in the London to Melbourne air race. Later it served as an experimental aircraft with the RAF. In 1937, it returned to its civilian registration and broke the England to Capetown record.

In 1951, G-ACSS had another brief moment of glory as the star exhibit in the aviation section of the Festival of Britain. Then she was forgotten until 1965. Now this beautiful aeroplane is the subject of the Shuttleworth Trust's most adventurous project – a £25,000 restoration programme.

In the not too distant future, air display visitors will thrill to the roar of twin Gypsy engines and to the sleek lines of the blood-red Comet Racer as she flashes overhead.

Old Warden lies near the A1/A1(M) motorway, in easy reach of London.

Zeppelin

Count Ferdinand von Zeppelin was one of the great figures of aviation history. He was also one of the most tragic. He had a dream of providing cheap, safe, fast transport for the mass of the people. For a few brief years that dream came true. The Count's beautiful silver ships made airline history at a time when the aeroplane was still a frail underpowered toy. Then came the First World War and the dream turned into a nightmare. Today the name *Zeppelin* conjures up pictures of aerial warfare in a bygone age: of the thunder of heavy guns and the scream of bombs; of searchlights crossing in the night sky, and of the great orange fireball as another giant airship plunged to destruction.

The story began on 2 July 1900, when LZ.1 (Luftschiff Zeppelin 1) lifted off from her floating hangar on Lake Constance. She carried five people on an eighteen-minute voyage. Despite engine and structural

above German Army Zeppelin LZ-77 shot down by French guns in 1916 below Zeppelin attacked by a BE-2C

problems she climbed to over 300 metres and flew at 20mph (32km/h).

Count Zeppelin built a number of ships with varying degrees of success and failure. Then, in 1910, he piloted LZ.7, the *Deutschland*, on a maiden 300 mile (480km) voyage with twenty passengers. *Deutschland* was ill-fated. On a later flight she flew into a violent storm and crashed in a forest, her crew and passengers escaping unharmed.

During the next four years *Deutschland*'s sister ships, the *Schwagon* and the *Victoria Louise* carried 5,577 passengers over routes totalling 21,700 miles (34,720km). It was the world's first airline service, and not a single passenger was killed or injured.

Then in 1914 came war. The airship factories began building machines to carry bombs instead of people. The Zeppelin was seen as the weapon of the future. Aeroplanes had made considerable strides since the Wright Flyer of 1903, but they were powerless in the face of the airship.

For more than a year the Zeppelins roamed unhindered through the night skies over England. Crowds on

the ground would watch the huge silvery 'cigars' caught in the cross of searchlights. The guns around London would thunder in protest, but the shells burst wide of their targets. Nothing could stop the big ships.

The tide began to turn on the night of 7 June 1915, when a young naval lieutenant, Reggie Warnford, destroyed airship LZ.37 over Belgium. Then, on 31 March, five airships set out for a routine raid over southern England. LZ.15 was hit by a shell and damaged over Dartford. The captain jettisoned bombs and ballast to turn for home but he was too late. Second Lieutenant Alfred de Bath Brandon, flying a BE2C, had seen LZ.15 caught in searchlights and was climbing to attack. A machine gun battle ensued between the vast airship and the tiny biplane. Brandon flew above LZ.15 scattering explosive darts and incendiary bombs.

The airship did not catch fire, but she was badly damaged. Gas was leaking from four gas bags. All heavy equipment including machine guns and engine covers was dumped overboard, but it was of no use. LZ.15 crashed in the sea and her crew were rescued by British trawlers.

The most famous Zeppelin fight happened on 2 September 1916. Twelve ships had set out to raid England. Climbing from his base near Hornchurch, Lieutenant Leefe Robinson saw LZ.98 illuminated by searchlights. He turned towards her, gaining height. At a height of 3,600 metres he attacked, firing his machine gun into her gas bags from bow to stern. As this seemed to have no effect he flew to one side and poured more ammunition into her. Again nothing happened. He flew under the huge bulk and fired upwards.

This time there was an orange glow, and then the stern of the airship exploded into flame. Far below, Londoners watched as LZ.98 plunged to the ground, ablaze from end to end. For his exploit Leefe Robinson won the Victoria Cross. His victory put new heart into London's defences, and Zeppelin losses began to mount. By the end of 1916 the military Zeppelin was as outdated as the brontosaurus, and the aeroplane ruled the sky.

UFO

What is a UFO? The description *unidentified flying object* was first used by United States Air Force officers who were involved in investigating the great flying saucer mystery of the late 40s. In June 1947, Kenneth Arnold, an American private pilot, reported seeing nine 'saucer shaped' objects flying in line astern between mountain peaks near Mount Ranier. Soon thousands of people all over the world were seeing flying saucers.

Their stories might have been filed away and forgotten except that some witnesses were highly trained observers – pilots, naval captains, scientists, engineers and astronomers.

The USA, Britain, France, Australia, Russia and the Argentine probed the mysterious UFOs. Occasionally government officials would state that flying saucers were natural objects, such as the planet Venus, meteorological balloons, shooting stars or 'sun dogs' (a reflection of the sun on ice clouds).

Unfortunately people kept seeing objects which did not fit in with the neat official explanations. The most dramatic incident came on 7 January 1948. Thousands of people in the state of Kentucky saw a huge circular object glowing alternately red and white. Police who alerted Fort Knox estimated the disc to be just over 76 metres in diameter.

The object approached Godman Air Force Base. Officers in the control tower, including the base commander, saw the UFO between gaps in the cloud. Three P-51 Mustang fighters, airborne on an exercise, were ordered to intercept.

One Mustang was piloted by Captain Thomas Mantell – a veteran of the Second World War. After a few minutes Mantell radioed: 'I can see it – it's tremendous – it's climbing away from me'. There was silence and then: 'It's still above me – I'm climbing to 6,000 metres'. Mantell was not heard from again. Later the wreckage of his fighter was found scattered in the desert. It had disintegrated in mid-air.

Although Kenneth Arnold began the present world-wide fascination with flying saucers, other men have

been reporting strange aerial objects since Ezekiel, in 593 BC, saw an aerial transport which he described as a 'wheel within a wheel'. It was 'the colour of Beryl [yellow/green] and there was fire and smoke like a whirlwind. On board the craft were beings with four faces and it was surrounded with rings full of eyes, which might have been portholes'.

There are other such stories in the Bible. Greek and Egyptian myth is full of aerial barges and flying heroes. Even further back, the Ramayana of ancient India describes aerial warships armed with frightful weapons. There are rays and bolts that sound like LASAR projectors, and a missile which destroyed an entire city, with its defending army.

Author's Note

Anybody who writes on the subject of UFOs must expect to be asked: 'Do you believe in flying saucers?' My answer has to be 'Yes'.

In 1943 I was a member of the Air Training Corps. Most cadets had heard rumours of fighters with jet or rocket propulsion. I was not too surprised, therefore, when I saw, late one evening, a bright light moving across the sky. It was the size of the full moon, oval in shape and fiery orange in colour. Droplets of fire seemed to drip from the main body to

form a short tapering tail. It crossed the sky silently, from horizon to horizon, in about eight seconds. I believed I had seen the test flight of a secret weapon.

Twenty years later, on 3 October 1963, I was at London Airport. With another photographer I had just completed an assignment in the cargo terminal. It was a 'dirty' night with rain and high wind. We were walking back to our car when I saw a circular object above us.

It was moving rapidly into wind below broken cloud. We could see the lights of the airfield reflected on its polished, metallic undersurface. As it moved away we could see that it was a disc – the shape of two saucers placed edge to edge. At an elevation of some 45° it banked and changed course, disappearing into the night.

The sighting lasted four or five seconds. There was no sound above the noise of the wind and no way to judge its size. My impression was of a large machine about the size of a Comet IV. Because it banked into its turn it seemed to me that it was 'flying' in the aerodynamic sense.

I have no theories about flying saucers. I only know what I saw.

Photograph taken by Stephen Darbishire in the Lake District

It can do anything

The scene is a forest clearing. Dawn light filters through the high branches. The silence is broken only by the chatter of birds welcoming a new day. Suddenly a bellow of noise puts the birds to flight. The sound rises to a crescendo and a bigger, deadlier bird takes to the air.

Rising vertically on shimmering columns of hot gas is a grey-green Harrier GR MK1. For a brief moment the Harrier hovers motionless above the tree tops. Then it accelerates away, streaking towards its target at a speed of 720mph (1,152km/h). The woodland glade has become a front-line airfield. The Harrier is one of a dozen scattered in clearings across almost 1.5 kilometres of woodland. It is engaged in a routine squadron exercise.

The Harrier is the first vertical-take-off/landing (VTOL) fighter bomber to go into service with any air force in the world. It can take off from an area the size of a tennis court with a ton of air-to-air and air-to-ground missiles. Alternatively, by making a short take-off run (STOL) it can use the lift generated by its wings to raise a load of almost 2,273kg.

The Harrier does not need the long concrete runways used by ordinary jet aircraft. Runways are easily found and destroyed by an enemy. That is what happened in the Arab-Israeli War of 1967. Israeli aircraft destroyed almost every military runway in Egypt. The Egyptian aircraft were unable to take off and were destroyed in hundreds by marauding Israeli fighter bombers.

Harrier's runways cannot be destroyed. Any woodland clearing, cricket pitch, farmyard or playground can become an airbase in a matter of minutes. Any short, straight stretch of second-class road – even a football pitch – can become a Harrier runway. When not actually taking off or landing, Harriers simply vanish into the countryside. Hidden under trees or in barns, they present an impossible target for enemy reconnaissance pilots.

The Harrier story goes back to 1957 when Sir Sydney Camm set out to design an experimental fighter around the revolutionary Bristol Pegasus turbojet. The Pegasus was unlike any previous jet engine. Its jet efflux was exhausted through four nozzles. The nozzles could be rotated through more than 90° to give 'vectored thrust'. This meant that the thrust of the engine could either be used for lift or for propulsion.

The new aircraft was designated P1127 and named Kestrel. It looked like an ordinary jet fighter except for the four jet nozzles mounted on the side of the fuselage below the wings. The pilot's controls also appeared conventional, except for the addition of a thrust lever to direct the nozzles backwards or downwards. Kestrel

also had four additional small jets – one under each wingtip and one under the nose and tail. These were connected to the control column and rudder pedals to roll and pitch the aircraft when forward speed was too low for the aerodynamic control surfaces to 'bite' the air.

The first Kestrel rolled out of the factory in October 1960. For several months she made conventional take-offs and landings on a long concrete runway. A few brief hovering flights were made close to the ground. Then, early in 1961, the flight test department decided that Kestrel was ready for her big test. This time she was going to 'translate' from vertical flight to forward flight and back again.

The pilot pointed the thrust nozzles at the ground and steadily opened the throttle. As power increased, Kestrel rocked gently from wheel to wheel. Then she lifted into the air. At a height of about 18 metres the pilot began very slowly to move the nozzles to the rear. Kestrel moved slowly forward. As her speed increased, the wings began to bite the air and generate lift. The nozzles swung further to the rear and Kestrel accelerated away, to appear a few minutes later in a high speed run across the airfield.

To land the Kestrel vertically, the pilot reversed the take-off procedure. As the aircraft approached the landing site, the nozzles were gradually rotated until they pointed straight down. As the aircraft decelerated, the wing lift was reduced. Gradually the weight of the machine was taken by the vertical thrust. When the machine was hovering, the pilot reduced power and the craft descended to touch down.

Kestrel was built to prove the practicability of the VTOL fighter. This it did, operating from tiny clearings and from the helicopter platforms of ships at sea. In 1965 nine Kestrels took part in a unique experiment. A 'tri-partite' squadron was formed with British, German and American pilots. Each aircraft carried an emblem combining the national markings of the RAF, the Luftwaffe and the USAF.

Although Kestrel was unique among military aircraft, it could carry only a very small warload. A much more powerful version with a new Rolls/Bristol Pegasus engine was ordered. Its name was to be Harrier. The new aircraft first flew in August 1967. It could lift up to two-and-a-half tons of bombs and rockets and fly at the speed of sound. The RAF ordered a hundred Harrier GR MK1s and a small number of Harrier T MK2 operational two-seat trainers. The US Marine Corps followed quickly with an order for another 110 Harrier AV-8As to provide close air support for Marine operations. Harriers are also on order for the Spanish Navy. More are expected to equip the new midget carriers under construction for both the British Royal Navy and the US Navy.

Although Harrier was designed as a ground attack aircraft, British and American service pilots have discovered that it has capabilities even its designers did not suspect. By using thrust vectoring in conjunction with aerodynamic controls at high speeds, pilots have performed incredible manoeuvres beyond the capabilities of orthodox fighters.

In secret combat trials Harriers have been able to outfight the most modern supersonic interceptors. They can be pulled into unbelievably tight turns, and they can stop almost dead in the air while a pursuer goes blundering past at a speed of 700mph (1,120km/h).

Harrier is the start of a new line of fighting aircraft. An 'Advanced Harrier' is already under development for the RAF, Royal Navy, US Navy and the US Marines. This advanced Harrier will have a still more powerful Pegasus 15 engine and a new low-drag wing.

The aeroplane which began the Harrier story, the P1127 Kestrel prototype, can be seen at the RAF Museum at Hendon in north London. It forms part of a display dedicated to the memory of one of Britain's greatest aircraft designers, Sir Sydney Camm. The aircraft that surround it read like a page in the history of aerial warfare: Hurricane, Typhoon, Tempest, Sea Fury and Hunter.

below left *Harrier firing rockets* below right *a Harrier comes in to land during an exercise in Westphalia, while another Harrier is towed into a camouflaged position*

How an aeroplane flies

'What keeps it up?' That is a question many people ask when they see a giant jetliner crossing the sky at 600mph (960km/h). A Boeing 747 Jumbo jet laden with 400 passengers weighs almost 350 tons at take-off. How is this aerial juggernaut supported by the same insubstantial gas that surrounds us every day?

In our homes the air is usually so still that we notice its presence only when a draught disturbs a curtain or causes a door to slam. But when air is in motion we call it wind. Then it can have very powerful effects. It can turn a windmill to pump water or generate electricity. It can drive an 800-ton windjammer across an ocean.

It is this great energy, controlled and harnessed by the science of *aerodynamics*, that lifts an aeroplane from the ground and supports it in flight. If you take a large sheet of cardboard out of doors on a windy day you will discover for yourself the first law of aerodynamics. As long as the sheet is edge on into the wind, you will be able to hold it without difficulty. Now try to hold it at an angle to the wind. A powerful force tears the sheet from your hands.

This force, which we call *lift*, was first understood by the ancient Chinese. They constructed huge kites for use in religious festivals. There is evidence that such kites could lift men high into the air. The way a kite works is shown in diagram 1. The string holds the kite in a stable position at a more or less constant angle to the wind or *airflow*. The angle at which the kite meets the airflow is called the *angle of attack*. On it depends the amount of lift produced by the surface of the kite. The greater the angle, up to a maximum of around 45°, the greater will be the lift.

Another force also acts upon the kite and this we call *drag*. Drag acts in the direction of the airflow. The pull we feel on a kite string is a combination of lift and drag. When the two forces are in balance, the kite will fly smoothly and steadily. The kite string acts as a *stabilizer*. It holds the kite at a constant angle of attack. If the kite string were to break, the kite would tumble over and over, out of control.

If, however, the kite were mounted on a pole and equipped with a second smaller kite to act as a stabilizer (see diagram 2) it would become a free-flying glider. This was discovered by Sir George Cayley in 1804. It was to become the basic principle of most early aeroplanes.

A kite usually has a single, flat flying surface. The section through this is called a *flat plate aerofoil*. You can prove for yourself that this simple form of wing works very well by constructing the easy-to-build glider described on page 66.

However, a modern aeroplane needs a far more efficient aerofoil. A typical modern wing section is shown in diagram 3. Part of the lift is produced in a similar way by the airflow meeting the lower surface of the wing at an angle. A greatly increased lifting force is produced by the shape of the aerofoil.

Notice the curved or *cambered* upper surface. Imagine two equal volumes of air meeting the front or *leading edge* of the wing and separating, one to pass over and one to pass under. The diagram shows that air moving over the upper surface has further to travel. This in turn means that a volume of air above the wing must occupy a greater space than a similar volume below the wing. When air expands to fill a greater space, its pressure is lowered.

In this way, when an aeroplane moves through the air, an area of low pressure is created above the entire wing surface. The higher pressure below the wing then pushes the aeroplane upwards.

As with a kite, the greater the angle of attack, the greater will be the lift generated – up to an angle of around 15°. At this point the smooth airflow over the wing suddenly breaks up and becomes *turbulent*. The lifting force is almost completely destroyed and the wing is said to have *stalled* (diagram 4).

We saw earlier how a kite was affected by drag. An aircraft wing, and in fact the entire aircraft structure or *airframe*, is similarly subject to drag. For this reason modern aeroplanes are *streamlined*. Streamlining means that the structure is designed to allow the

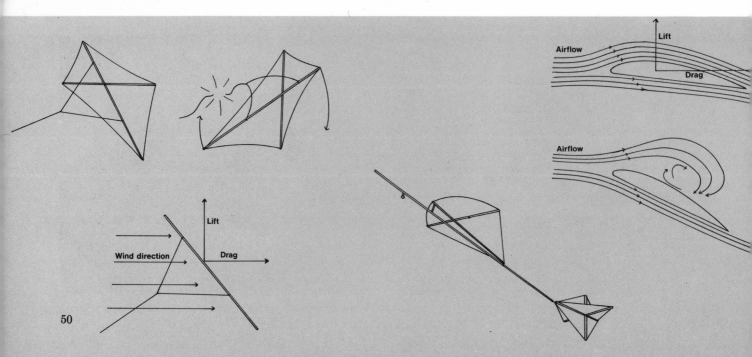

machine to move through the air with the smallest possible disturbance of the airflow. The undercarriage is usually retracted and covered. The wings and tail surfaces are smoothed into the body or *fuselage* with *fairings* or *fillets* which reduce turbulence.

Even the rivets are *countersunk* so that the rivet head is flush with the surface. Special paints or *dopes* are used to give a smooth glossy finish which further reduces air resistance. The pilots of racing aircraft will even wax their machines to gain an extra 5 or 10mph (8 or 16km/h).

On pages 52 and 53 we see a typical modern jet aeroplane. It is the BAC Strikemaster, which can be employed either as a ground attack aircraft or as a two-seat trainer. The drawing illustrates the position of the control surfaces and other vital parts.

Ailerons are moveable surfaces on the *trailing edge* of the wing near to the *wing tip*. They are coupled together so that when one rises, the other is depressed. When the pilot moves the control column to the left, the left aileron is raised while the righthand aileron is lowered. Depressing an aileron increases the angle of attack of that part of the wing and thus results in an increase in lift. When an aileron is raised, the angle of attack is decreased and the lifting force is reduced. Thus when the control column is moved to the left, lift is increased on the righthand wing and decreased on the lefthand wing. This effect causes the aeroplane to *roll* or *bank* to the left.

In the same manner, moving the control column to the right will cause the machine to roll to the right.

To make an aeroplane turn the pilot uses the ailerons together with the *rudder*, which is the moveable section of the vertical tail surface. The fixed part of the vertical tail surface is called the *fin*. To turn to the left the pilot moves the control column to the left and, at the same time, presses his foot on the left rudder pedal. This causes the rudder surface to move to the left.

You will understand how the rudder works if you think of the fin and rudder together as a small wing mounted in a vertical position on the rear fuselage. When the rudder moves to the left it gives the whole surface a positive angle of attack and causes a lifting force to the right. This makes the rear of the fuselage move to the right and at the same time pushes or *yaws* the nose of the aircraft to the left. Similarly, pressure on the right rudder pedal will move the rudder to the right and cause the nose of the aeroplane to yaw to the right.

A pilot could use rudder only to make a turn, but the aircraft would *skid* towards the outside of the turn like a car on an icy road. This would be uncomfortable for passengers who would feel themselves pushed to the side by *centrifugal force*. Similarly, it is possible to use ailerons only to make a turn, but in this case the aircraft would *sideslip* into the centre of the turning circle.

To make a *balanced turn*, the pilot

uses aileron and rudder together. Diagram 4 illustrates such a turn. The weight of the aeroplane (and of the passengers) is acting at right angles to the cabin floor, just as in normal flight, and the passengers feel no sensation of turning.

The other important control surface is the elevator. This is a moveable flap at the trailing edge of the *tailplane* or stabilizer. When the control column is pushed forward the elevator is depressed. This increases the angle of attack of the tailplane, thus increasing its lift. The rear of the fuselage is raised and the nose is lowered. Similarly, pulling back the control column raises the nose.

In addition to the basic aerodynamic controls, the pilot has a number of *high-lift* devices which increase the camber of the aerofoil section and, in some cases, increase the area of the wing. These *slats*, *droop leading edges*, *slots* and *flaps* are illustrated in diagram 5. Their purpose is to increase the lift of the wing and to delay the onset of the stall. This allows the aircraft to fly safely at low speeds and greatly reduces the distances required for take-off and landing. The development of such devices has helped to make flying one of the safest methods of travel.

We have seen how aerodynamic forces act upon an aeroplane in flight. To thrust that aeroplane into the air and keep it flying we need power, as explained on page 74.

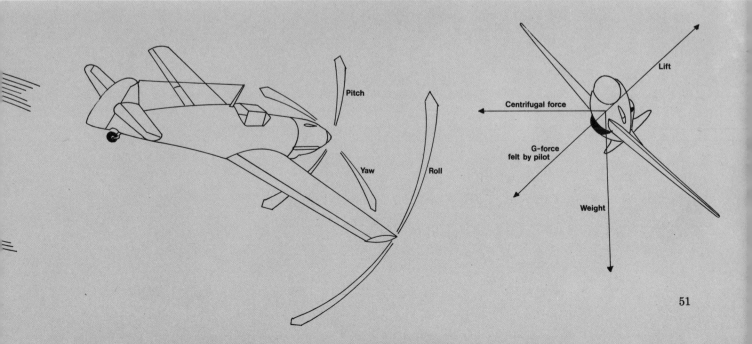

BAC Strikemaster

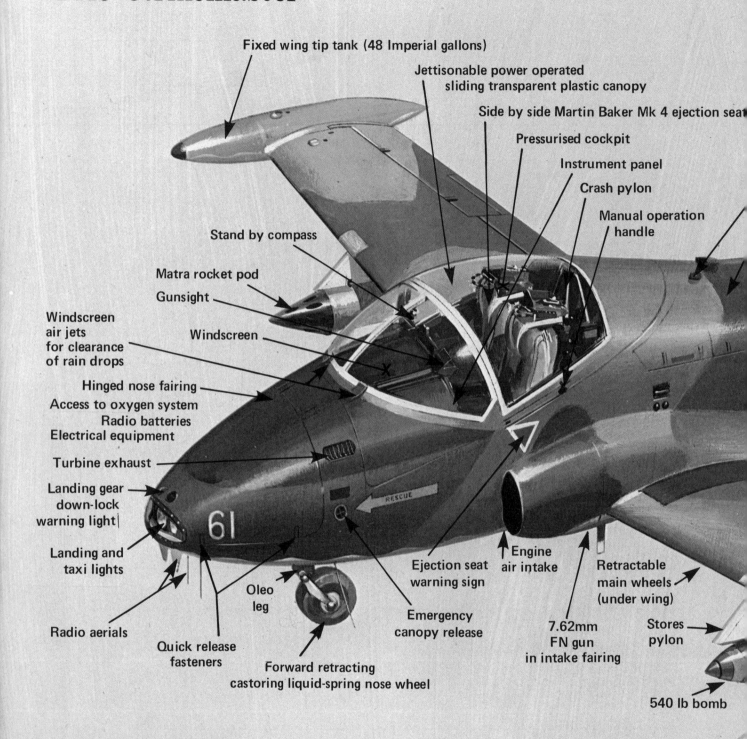

Fixed wing tip tank (48 Imperial gallons)

Jettisonable power operated
sliding transparent plastic canopy

Side by side Martin Baker Mk 4 ejection seat

Pressurised cockpit

Instrument panel

Crash pylon

Manual operation
handle

Stand by compass

Matra rocket pod

Gunsight

Windscreen
air jets
for clearance
of rain drops

Windscreen

Hinged nose fairing

Access to oxygen system
Radio batteries
Electrical equipment

Turbine exhaust

Landing gear
down-lock
warning light

Landing and
taxi lights

Radio aerials

Quick release
fasteners

Oleo
leg

Forward retracting
castoring liquid-spring nose wheel

Ejection seat
warning sign

Emergency
canopy release

Engine
air intake

Retractable
main wheels
(under wing)

7.62mm
FN gun
in intake fairing

Stores
pylon

540 lb bomb

PARTS OF AN AEROPLANE

BRITISH AIRCRAFT CORPORATION BAC 167 STRIKEMASTER
DUAL PURPOSE GROUND ATTACK AIRCRAFT AND PILOT TRAINER

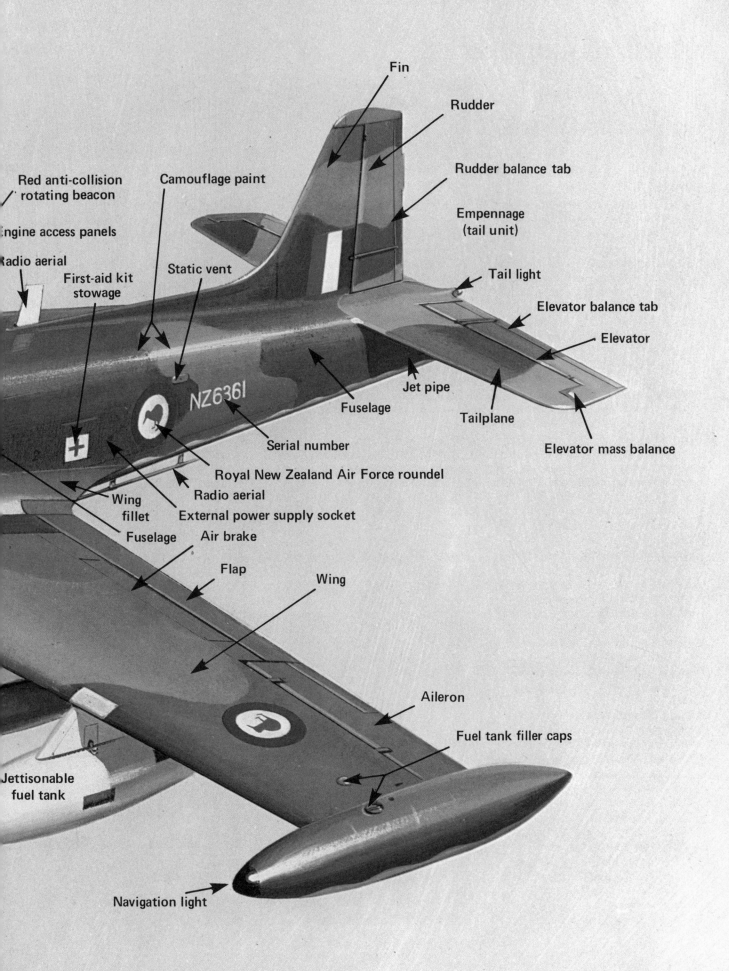

Fin

Rudder

Rudder balance tab

Empennage
(tail unit)

Camouflage paint

Red anti-collision
rotating beacon

Engine access panels

Radio aerial

First-aid kit
stowage

Static vent

Tail light

Elevator balance tab

Elevator

Jet pipe

Fuselage

Tailplane

Elevator mass balance

NZ6361

Serial number

Royal New Zealand Air Force roundel

Radio aerial

Wing
fillet

External power supply socket

Fuselage

Air brake

Flap

Wing

Aileron

Fuel tank filler caps

Jettisonable
fuel tank

Navigation light

Aerial filling station

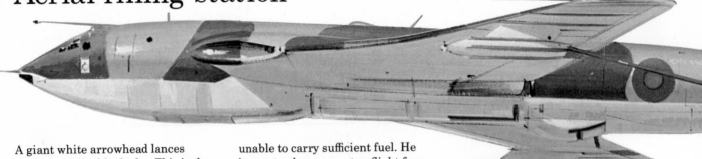

A giant white arrowhead lances across the blue-black sky. This is the Rockwell B-1A supersonic swingwing bomber. A low arctic sun shades the gleaming white wings with gold. Ten miles (16km) below, curving banks of amber cloud mask the northern ice fields. The big bomber is short of fuel. Far ahead a KB135 tanker cruises on station. Rendezvous is only minutes away.

Air brakes swing open and the B-1A decelerates, dropping fast into the denser atmosphere of the tropopause. Slowly the great wings swing forward to bite the air. As she decelerates across the sound barrier, strange patterns of moisture flicker around her. B-1A is no longer an arrowhead, her long graceful wings now span almost 42 metres.

Now the tanker is in sight. The two machines close rapidly to formate with the bomber's needle nose tucked under the tanker's tail. The telescopic refuelling boom of the KB135 swings slowly down, two small aerofoils guiding the nozzle towards the fuel socket above the bomber's nose. Suddenly a telescopic probe in the tip of the boom slams home and the two machines are locked together. In seconds tons of fuel are pouring into the B-1A's cavernous tanks....

Refuelling an aeroplane in flight began as a 'barnstorming' stunt in America in August 1923 when two USAAF Lieutenants, L. H. Smith and J. P. Richter, remained airborne in a DH-4B for more than thirty-seven hours. Their refuelling procedure involved a weighted line trailed by the tanker and caught in a hooked stick by the receiving aircrew.

The method may have been crude, but pioneering British airman Alan Cobham saw the possibilities. He had made many epic long-range flights and well knew the problem of being unable to carry sufficient fuel. He began to plan a non-stop flight from England to Australia. The aircraft, a single-engined Airspeed Courier, would be refuelled from flying tankers stationed along the route.

During trials the Courier was refuelled successfully many times from a Handley Page W10 airliner. The method was still elementary. The tanker trailed a line weighted with a water-filled rubber bag – a much safer ballast than the lead-filled paint cans of earlier tests. The line was caught by the second crewman of the Courier standing half out of the aircraft through a sliding roof.

The England to Australia flight began on 22 September 1934. The aircraft fuelled in the air over Portsmouth and then flew to Malta where a second refuelling took place. Sadly, a mechanical fault, unconnected with the refuelling equipment, led to the flight being abandoned.

Despite the disappointment, Alan Cobham persevered. He formed a company called Flight Refuelling Ltd, and carried out many more successful experiments. Imperial Airways ordered four of their new C Class Empire flying boats to be equipped for aerial refuelling. In August 1939 the first transatlantic service was inaugurated. The big C boats took off with fuel tanks half empty. Once airborne, they would take on more than three tons of fuel from a converted Harrow bomber.

Once more, however, unforeseen circumstances snatched away success. After three weeks war was declared and the service ended. Surprisingly, little use was made of flight refuelling techniques during

Aircrew inspect the refuelling drogue of a Handley Page Victor K2 aircraft

the war, but interest was revived with the coming of the jet engine. Early jet fighters were so thirsty that they could remain airborne for less than an hour.

Flight Refuelling Ltd developed the 'probe and drogue' system. The tanker trailed a fuel pipe which ended in a cone-shaped drogue. The receiving aircraft was equipped with a probe which had to be flown into the drogue and locked into place. After refuelling, the probe was

unlocked and the machines separated.

The RAF adopted the probe and drogue system. So did the Russian Air Force and the US Navy. The USAF developed its own 'flying telescopic boom' method, the boom being flown into position by a crewman aboard the tanker.

Today aerial refuelling is just a routine procedure. The endurance of military aircraft is limited only by the stamina of the aircrews. In 1969 an RAF Harrier VTOL fighter won

the great transatlantic air race with the aid of a Victor tanker. The flight began in a coalyard behind St Pancras station in London and ended on a wharf in New York. Even more remarkable was a flight by a Lockheed SR-71A strategic reconnaissance aircraft in 1971. With the aid of KB 135 tankers spaced along its route the SR-71A covered 15,000 miles (24,000km) at Mach 3, an average speed of more than 2,000mph (3,200km/h).

C Class Empire flying boat being refuelled from a converted Harrow bomber

How a helicopter flies

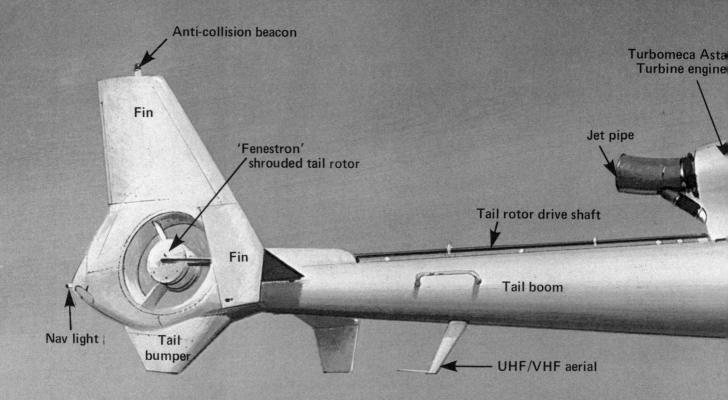

Anti-collision beacon

Fin

'Fenestron'
shrouded tail rotor

Fin

Nav light

Tail
bumper

Turbomeca Asta
Turbine engine

Jet pipe

Tail rotor drive shaft

Tail boom

UHF/VHF aerial

The secret of helicopter flight is to be found in the rotor. A helicopter rotor is made up of two or more long narrow wings rotating about a central axis. These rotor blades generate lift in exactly the same way as the wings of a fixed-wing aeroplane. That is, by moving through the air at a positive angle of attack (see 'How an Aeroplane Flies'). The big difference between a helicopter and a fixed-wing machine is that the rotating wings can develop sufficient lift for take-off without the need for a take-off run.

The principle of the rotating wing was known to Leonardo da Vinci and to Cayley. Development of the helicopter, however, was much less rapid than that of fixed-wing aircraft. One reason for this was the problem of stability.

When a helicopter rotor is tilted,

the machine moves in the direction of the tilt. This is how horizontal flight is achieved. Horizontal flight, however, poses a problem. Consider a rotor turning in a clockwise direction (seen from above), with the helicopter in forward flight. Blades in the left-hand side of the rotor disc are moving forward (relative to the direction of flight), while blades in the right-hand side of the disc are moving backwards.

This means that the airspeed of the left-hand (advancing) blade is increased by the airspeed of the helicopter. The speed of the right-hand (retreating) blade is decreased by a similar amount. The faster a wing moves through air the greater its lift. The advancing segment of a helicopter rotor disc in horizontal flight develops more lift than the retreating segment. The effect is to

roll the helicopter to the right. The solution is to vary the angle of attack (pitch) of the blades as they move around the rotor head. The angle of attack of advancing blades is automatically reduced while that of retreating blades is increased. This balances lift across the disc.

'Torque' presents another problem. Torque is a force which tends to turn the fuselage in the opposite direction to the rotor. Most helicopters have a vertical tail rotor to counteract torque and to provide directional control. In other machines torque is cancelled out by having two contra-rotating rotors. These may be mounted on either side of the fuselage (Mi-12), at either end of the fuselage (Boeing Vertol), or one above the other rotating around the same axis (KAMOV 25).

WESTLAND AEROSPATIALE SA 341 GAZELLE

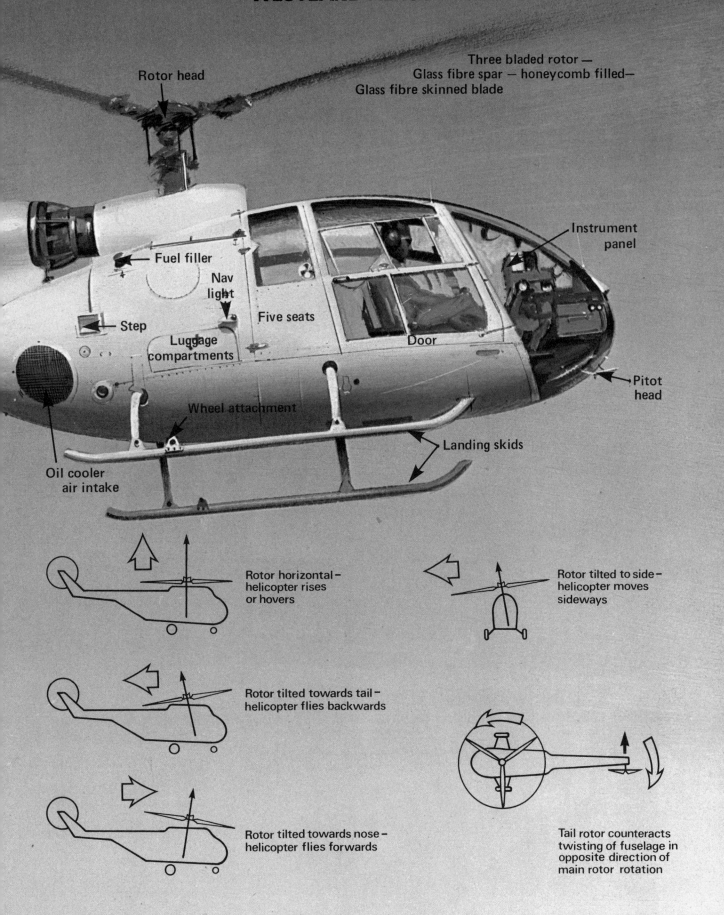

Rotor head

Three bladed rotor —
Glass fibre spar — honeycomb filled—
Glass fibre skinned blade

Fuel filler

Nav
light

Five seats

Step

Luggage
compartments

Door

Instrument
panel

Pitot
head

Wheel attachment

Landing skids

Oil cooler
air intake

Rotor horizontal-
helicopter rises
or hovers

Rotor tilted to side-
helicopter moves
sideways

Rotor tilted towards tail-
helicopter flies backwards

Rotor tilted towards nose-
helicopter flies forwards

Tail rotor counteracts
twisting of fuselage in
opposite direction of
main rotor rotation

Sikorsky R-4, a versatile two-seat helicopter

Helicopters at work

A helicopter about to land on an oil rig in the North Sea

The first practicable helicopter was the two-seat Sikorsky R-4. Although it was a small machine with a limited payload, its special capabilities were quickly appreciated. R-4 served with both American and British forces in 1944–5. It flew anti-submarine and rescue patrols operating from tiny improvised platforms aboard ships at sea. In the front line it was used for observation and the transport of vital personnel and equipment. One R-4 pilot rescued an airman who had been shot down behind enemy lines. This action foreshadowed the future life-saving role of helicopters in both peace and war.

In the Korean and Vietnamese wars, rescue of airmen downed behind enemy lines became routine. Even more important was the part played by helicopters in evacuating wounded from the front line and flying them directly to military hospitals. Thousands of men owe their lives to crews who flew repeatedly into battle zones regardless of their own safety.

Inevitably the helicopter itself became a weapon of war. In Vietnam 'airborne cavalry' units replaced the parachute brigades of other wars. Vast numbers of Bell 'Huey Choppers' carried troops to and from the battle field. Other helicopters

The Bell Hueycobra, a specialized helicopter gunship

were armed with machine guns and rockets. In hill and jungle terrain armed helicopters proved more effective than fixed-wing machines. The next step was a specialized helicopter gunship, the Hueycobra. The Bell Hueycobra has a speed of 220mph (352km/h) and a warload of multi-barrel cannons, grenade launchers and anti-tank missiles.

In more peaceful areas helicopters continue with their life-saving role. Rescue choppers are a common sight in coastal areas, ready to give instant aid to yachtsmen or bathers in trouble. Other helicopters have rescued entire crews from sinking ships and blazing oil rigs, or braved heat and smoke to snatch people from the tops of burning buildings.

Helicopters are playing a vital role in industry and commerce. Scheduled airline services operate from city centres carrying up to twenty-eight passengers at 130mph (208km/h). 'Flying cranes' carry heavy power cables across rivers and valleys, and lift building sections weighing many tons into position high above the ground.

Some industries, such as off-shore oil, are almost completely dependent upon helicopters for the supply and maintenance of drilling rigs. The demand is for even bigger and more powerful machines. The giant Russian Mil Mi-12 has already lifted a record load of forty tons to a height of over 2,133 metres. That is the equivalent of a fully loaded bus, or a passenger compartment accommodating 250 people.

59

The Schneider Trophy

The crackling roar of a Rolls-Royce 'R' engine echoed across the Solent. It heralded the approach of a Supermarine S-6B. At a speed of 400mph (640km/h) the tiny blue and silver floatplane streaked low over the water to cross the finishing line at Ryde, Isle of Wight. The year was 1931. As he flashed past the cheering crowds on the sea-front the pilot, Flight Lieutenant Boothman, knew he had won the Schneider Trophy outright for Great Britain.

The trophy was created in 1912 by M. Jacques Schneider. He wanted to encourage the development of marine aircraft. The rules were simple. The aircraft were to fly a course of at least 150 miles (240km). The winning country would hold the trophy for a year and act as host for the next contest. Any country taking first place in three successive contests would win the trophy outright.

The first contest was held in Monaco in 1913 and was won by a Frenchman in a Deperdussin Racer. The Deperdussin was ahead of its time – a mid-wing monoplane with a finely streamlined fuselage.

Britain won the second contest with a Sopwith Tabloid biplane at an average speed of 88.5mph (141.6km/h). The date was 20 April 1914, and the return match was to be delayed five years by the First World War.

On 10 September 1919 the setting for the third contest was Bournemouth. The event was spoiled by a heavy mist. Only one entry, an Italian Savoia flying boat, completed the course. Unfortunately the pilot missed a turning point in fog and was disqualified. It was a gallant try,

however, and other contestants agreed that Italy should hold the trophy for a year.

The next two contests were held in Venice, and both of them were won by Italy. In 1920 the winner was a Savoia S-19 flying boat, while in 1921 it was a Macchi M-7 flying boat.

Venice was the setting once more in 1922. The Italians entered S-19 and M-7 flying boats, while Britain challenged with a Supermarine Sea-Lion flying boat. A very close contest was won by the Sea-Lion at just over 145.7mph (232.8km/h).

Britain's win brought the contest to Cowes on the Isle of Wight in 1923. British and French teams were equipped with flying boats while the United States entered two sleek Curtiss Navy Racers. One of these planes won with an average speed of approximately 177.3mph (282km/h).

This meant that in 1925 the contest was held in America. This was the last year that flying boats competed, and they were hopelessly outclassed. The Schneider Trophy had become a contest for specialized racing machines. A notable entry was the British Supermarine S-4, a pretty mid-wing monoplane that was the first ancestor of the Spitfire. Sadly, S-4 crashed during trials and the contest was won by a Curtiss Army Racer at a speed of 232.5mph (372km/h).

In 1926 only Italy opposed the Americans with a Macchi M-39

low-wing monoplane. M-39 proved its superiority over the Curtiss biplanes. It won at a little over 246.4mph (394km/h) and henceforth monoplanes were to dominate the Schneider Trophy.

The contest returned to Venice in 1927. The RAF formed a special High Speed Flight to enter two Supermarine S-5s and a Gloster IVB biplane. Italy entered three Macchi M-52s. What began as a fiercely contested race was marred by mechanical failure. All three Macchis and the Gloster withdrew, leaving the two S-5s to 'fly-over' unopposed. The fastest, piloted by Flt. Lt. Webster, clocked 281.6mph (450.6km/h).

It was now decided to compete at two year intervals, and in 1929 the contest returned to the Isle of Wight. Although the French and American teams had to withdraw, the competition was fierce. The Italian team had two Macchi M-67s and a Macchi M-52. Britain put up two Supermarine S-6s and an S-5. The S-6s were powered by special Rolls-Royce 'R' engines of 1,900hp.

Tens of thousands of people lined the Solent. The blood-red Macchis began in cracking style, but soon bad luck was plaguing the Italians yet again. Both M-67s fell out, leaving the old M-52 to battle on alone.

Once again victory went to Britain

The Italian Macchi M.39, the machine that won the Schneider Trophy in 1926, over 50 years ago

The Supermarine S5, which came third in the Trophy race of 1929

with an average speed of almost 328.6mph (526km/h). The M-52 came second, with the S-5 third. The other S-6 was disqualified. Britain, therefore, needed only one more victory to win the trophy outright, but a short-sighted British government withdrew financial support. At the last moment Lady Houston gave £100,000 to pay for Britain's entry in 1931.

The date fixed for the race was 12 September. French and Italian teams were expected to compete, but both had to withdraw. Flt. Lt. Boothman was left to 'fly-over' in his new S-6B. The Rolls-Royce 'R' engine had been boosted to 2,350hp and the aircraft's average speed over a 200 mile (320km) course was just over 340mph (544km/h). The Schneider Trophy had come to Britain to stay and it may be seen at the Royal Aero Club in London.

Britain won much more than just a trophy, however. The Supermarine designer, R. J. Mitchell, later converted the sleek lines of the S-6B into the shape of the immortal Spitfire, and the Rolls-Royce 'R' engine became the Merlin, the power plant not only of the Spitfire and Hurricane, but also of the Mosquito, Mustang, Halifax and Lancaster.

top and bottom of the page: *the famous Supermarine S6B, which was the winner of the Trophy in 1931. This success meant that England had managed to win the Trophy outright*

David's first flying lesson

David's Tiger Moth taxied to the downwind boundary. It rolled to a stop, engine ticking over. On the fence a runway marker read '01', indicating that the runway direction was 010°. In the front cockpit David sat on two cushions so that he could see above the fuselage. His flying jacket was just a little too large. On his head he wore a leather helmet and goggles. Cables from the helmet earphones were plugged into a socket at the side of the cockpit.

David was excited. He had flown before, but today he was going to have his first flying lesson. Over the 'intercom' he could hear his father in the rear cockpit calling the cockpit checks aloud. 'T – trim...central. T – throttle friction nut...tight. M – mixture...rich. F – fuel ...tap on and sufficient fuel for flight. S – slats... unlocked. H – harness...tight. H – hatches...closed. O – oil pressure... normal'. David knew that the checks are remembered by the initial letters: T T M F S H H O. He also knew that

failure to check any one of these items could lead to an accident.

Clear for take-off

'Can you hear me David? Are your straps tight?' His father's voice echoed over the intercom.

'Loud and clear, Dad. Straps are all tight.'

'Good. Control are giving us a "green". That means we are clear to take off. I want you to hold the control column lightly with the finger tips of your right hand and rest your feet gently on the rudder pedals. Just follow my movements and notice what happens to the aeroplane.'

David glanced towards the control tower and saw the steady green light of an Aldis lamp. His father spoke again.

'No aircraft in the circuit – all clear above and behind.'

The throttle lever on the left side of the cockpit moved forward and the engine roared. David felt the left

rudder pedal move forward. The little biplane began to roll, swinging to the left and lining up into wind on runway 01.

'Right – off we go.'

The throttle opened wide and the Tiger bounded forward over the grass. David felt himself thrust back in his seat. The stick moved forward a little and he felt the tail lift. Now he could see over the nose. The hangars and trees on the upwind boundary seemed to be rushing to meet them.

He felt the rudder pedals move as his father corrected a swing to the right. A glance at the ASI (Air Speed Indicator) showed the airspeed at 40mph (64km/h), and rising. There was a very slight backward pressure on the stick and he felt the wheels drumming the grass. For a moment the wheels left the ground, touched briefly again, and then they were airborne.

David felt the stick move forward slightly. His father said:

'I'm holding her down until we have climbing speed.'

David looked at the ASI. As the needle reached 65mph (104km/h) the stick moved back. Now the Tiger climbed rapidly. The tops of the trees on the upwind boundary slid past 76m below.

To the right David could see sunlight glinting on flooded gravel pits and beyond, the haze of the city. To his left farm and woodland stretched to the horizon. Below, village houses grew smaller and smaller as the Tiger Moth climbed.

Alone in the front cockpit, his hands and feet following the movements of the controls, it was easy to imagine that he was on his first solo flight. Then, once more his father's voice crackled from the back seat and the illusion was gone immediately.

'We'll go over to westward to find some open country. We don't want to disturb people on a Sunday morning.'

The Tiger banked gently to the left and steadied on her new course still climbing. The altimeter showed 750m and the needle kept up a steady clockwise movement. At 1,200m the ground seemed a very long way away. Greens and browns merged into a giant patchwork, fading to a hazy blue at the horizon.

Effect of controls – elevator

As they levelled off at 1,500m David
felt very glad that his father had
made him wear an extra sweater
under the flying jacket. So high above
the surface the air was bitterly cold,
even on a bright spring morning such
as this one. His father was speaking
again.

'First lesson is "effect of controls".
We'll begin with the elevator. At the
moment we are in straight and level
flight. Notice the position of the nose
a little below the horizon. That is how
we judge our speed. If the nose is kept
there we will cruise along nicely at
about 80mph (130km/h). It's no use
watching the ASI, we must keep
almost all our attention outside the
cockpit, with just an occasional
glance at the instruments. Now see
what happens when I push the stick
forward.'

David's hand moved with the
control column. He saw the nose drop
further and further below the
horizon. The noise of the slipstream

in the flying wires increased. He
glanced at the ASI. The needle
showed 95mph (152km/h) and it was
rising. The altimeter needle passed
the 1,400m mark and spiralled
downward.

'I'm going to level off now,'
continued David's father.

The stick moved firmly back and
the nose came up. The noise of the
wind lessened and the nose steadied
in the cruise position below the
horizon. The altimeter showed
1,350m.

'I am pulling back on the stick.'

David watched the nose rise above
the horizon. The noise of the wind
grew less. A glance at the ASI
showed 65mph (104km/h). The
altimeter recorded a slow gain of
height.

'And now we'll try a stall.'

David wasn't sure if he would like
this, but he knew that stalling was
something every pilot must practise.
If a stall happens accidentally, he
must take corrective action without

even thinking about it.

The throttle lever moved back to
the fully closed position. The roar of
the engine died away and the
propeller slowed until it could be
seen flickering above the nose. The
stick came further back and the nose
rose higher.

With a bang the leading edge slats
fell open, feeding air over the wing
and delaying the stall. Still the stick
moved back and now the rush of the
slipstream died right away. The
aircraft seemed to wallow with her
nose pointed to the sky.

'We're just at the point of stalling,
David. The airflow over the wings is
so slow that the ailerons have little
effect.' To prove his point David's
father moved the control column
from side to side but the Tiger only
wallowed in response.

'Ease back on the stick with me.'

David dropped his eyes
momentarily to the ASI. The needle
was flickering above 40mph (64km/h).
A little shudder went through the

machine, and suddenly the nose was dropping...down...down...down. David felt a falling sensation clutch briefly at the pit of his stomach, like going down the steep slope of a roller-coaster. Then they were diving towards the fields far below.

As the nose dropped the stick went forward and the motor roared. Back on the stick again, and the biplane eased smoothly out of the dive.

'That wasn't too bad, was it? Now we will go back up to 1,500m and try the effect of ailerons.'

Effect of controls – ailerons

At 1,500m they levelled off.

'See what happens when we push the stick to left without moving the rudder pedals.'

The stick moved, and at once the Tiger rolled to the left. When the wings were at about 30° to the horizon the stick came back slightly towards centre.

David's father went on: 'I'm holding the bank steady. Notice what is happening.'

David felt the slipstream on the left side of his face. That meant that they were sideslipping. Then he saw that the nose was moving around the horizon to the left.

'The first effect of aileron is to roll the aircraft. The secondary effect is a sideslip which causes the nose to turn or yaw in the direction of the lowered wing. As you can see, the same thing happens when we move the stick over to the right.'

This time the Tiger rolled to the right, and after a moment the nose began to track to the right.

Effect of controls – rudder

They resumed level flight.

'The first effect of rudder is to yaw the nose in the direction of the rudder. Left foot forward, nose yaws to left. Right foot forward, nose yaws to right.'

As his father spoke, David noticed that the rudder pedals moved back and forth and the nose tracked first one way and then the other.

'Now see what happens if we hold on full left rudder.' The nose tracked to the left and David felt the slipstream on the right side of his face. They were skidding out of the turn. After a moment he noticed that

the Tiger was rolling to the left.

'The secondary effect of rudder is to roll the aircraft in the direction of the yaw. Imagine you're looking down on the aircraft. By yawing to the left we swing the right wing faster than the left. The faster the airflow over a wing the greater the lift. So the right wing comes up and we roll to the left.'

Effect of controls – the balanced turn

'To make an accurate turn we use aileron and rudder together, balancing sideslip with skid so that they cancel out.'

David felt the stick move to the right and the right rudder pedal move forward. The Tiger rolled to the right, the nose tracking smoothly around the horizon. This time there was no sensation of sideways movement.

'Look at the Turn and Bank Indicator, David.'

The Turn and Bank Indicator was a dial in the centre of the dashboard. It had two needles like the hands of a clock: one up and one down. The scale at the top showed sideslip or skid while the lower one indicated 'rate of turn'. Now the upper needle pointed to the zero mark. The lower pointer was on the 2 indicating a 'rate 2' or gentle turn.

'You have control'

'David, I'm going to take my hands and feet off the controls. Don't worry about the throttle. Just try to keep us straight and level. OK? You have control now!'

Suddenly David felt very alone in the front seat. Almost at once the nose dropped and he pulled back on

the stick. Now the nose reared up and the horizon had disappeared. Everything went quiet. Certain that they were about to stall he pushed the stick forward and once more they were diving.

David had been told about 'over controlling'. He forced himself to ease gently back on the stick and gradually lift the nose up to its cruising position below the horizon. He concentrated so hard on positioning the nose that he failed to notice the right wing dropping.

'Pick up the right wing, David.'

David suddenly realized that they were banked hard over and pushed the stick in the opposite direction. The Tiger rolled hard over to the left. Almost before he knew it they were in a steep left turn and the nose was dropping into a spiral dive.

David remembered again about over controlling. With small movements of the controls he brought the Tiger back to straight and level flight. The nose settled below the distant blue-grey line. He picked a patch of woodland that showed above the nose, as an aiming mark. For several minutes the Tiger flew on straight and level, her new pilot quickly gaining confidence in both the aircraft and himself.

'That was well done, David.'

He had almost forgotten his father in the back seat.

'OK. I've got control again now. Next time you can try some turns.'

Spinning

'Dad, can we do a spin before we go back?'

'Yes, if you want to. I'll climb back up to 1,500m.'

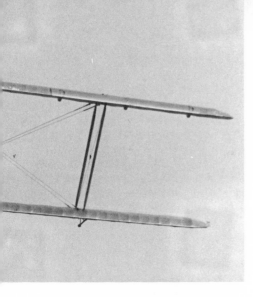

The engine roared and the Tiger nosed up into the climb.

'David, make sure your straps are tight and the maps are stowed away.'

David checked everything was secure. 'All ready, Dad,' he said.

The Tiger levelled off at 1,500m on an easterly course. David could see the sun glinting on the gravel pits far ahead.

'Right. Hands and feet lightly on the controls, and follow my movements.'

The Tiger rolled into a steep turn to the left. David was pressed down into his seat. The wings seemed to be almost vertical and the turn and bank needle showed a rate 4 turn. They turned through 360° until the gravel pits were ahead once more. Then the aircraft snapped over into a rate 4 turn to the right. Again they kept turning until the glint of sun on water was above the nose.

'That was a rate 4 figure of eight, David. Apart from being fun, it gives me a clear view below to make sure there are no other aircraft about.'

'Slats...locked, Harness...tight, Hatches...closed.' David's father called the checks aloud. 'Right. Here we go.' The throttle lever moved back to the stop and the roar of the engine died away. The stick came back and the nose climbed high above the horizon. Again the Tiger was hanging almost motionless in the sky.

Then the stick moved to the right and the left rudder pedal was pushed forward. What happened next was almost too fast for David to follow. The Tiger rolled rapidly over to the left almost onto her back. There was that clutching feeling again in his middle.

For a moment he saw green fields swirling round and round above his head and then the nose was dropping down...down...down. The fields were below again now but the nose was still rotating to the left.

Once the aircraft was established in the spin the sensation was not particularly unpleasant. David was almost beginning to enjoy it when his father said: 'OK, it's time we recovered.'

The stick centralized and moved right forward. Full right rudder, and almost at once the rotation stopped. Smoothly the stick came back to ease the aircraft out of her dive.

'Look at the altimeter, David.' The needle showed 1,286m. 'We lost over 210m in that spin; that's why we must never stall or spin close to the ground. Now we'll go home and try a landing.'

Approach and landing

The Tiger swung around to the east until the gravel pits again showed above the nose. Gradually she lost height and soon they were running past the airfield at some 300m.

'The wind is in the north today, David, which means a righthand circuit. We vary the circuit according to the wind direction to reduce noise level for people on the ground.'

They turned to fly south directly over the centre of the field. Then they turned right again to join the southern leg of the circuit pattern. 'The circuit is actually a square path which takes us all the way around the field,' said David's father.

Three turns later they were flying downwind along the eastern boundary. 'Time for pre-landing checks. M – mixture...fully rich. T – throttle friction nut...loose. F – fuel ...fuel tap on and sufficient for circuit. S – slats...unlocked.'

The airfield dropped back under the right wing. The throttle came back and the engine note dropped to a low roar. A glance at the ASI showed 70mph (112km/h) as the Tiger banked gently to the right. Now they were parallel to the downwind fence. Another gentle turn to the right and they were lined up on Runway 01.

The throttle lever came back still further and the speed dropped to 60mph (96km/h). The green turf and bunkers of the golf course came up to meet them. David could see golfers shading their eyes to watch. Trees and bushes flashed by under the wings. The fence was coming up fast.

The throttle lever moved forward a little and the motor growled in response as his father made a slight correction for height. Then the fence whipped past under the wheels.

The throttle came all the way back. His father's voice was saying: 'Gently back on the stick.' The nose came up and the rush of the slipstream dropped away.

'Back, back on the stick, all the way back.'

David could feel the control column pressing against him. The Tiger seemed almost to hang in the air. Then the wheels and tail skid were drumming on the grass.

'Not a bad three-pointer,' his father said. 'Maybe next time I'll show you a loop.'

Aeromodelling

plastercine weight — wing support

Aeromodelling is great fun. It is also the way to learn about flying. The balsa wood gliders on this page are simple for a beginner. They need 1/32, 1/16 and 1/8 balsa (sheets of 36 in × 3¼ in), a model knife, steel ruler, large tube of balsa cement and a flat wooden surface plus a thick cardboard cutting board to protect the work surface

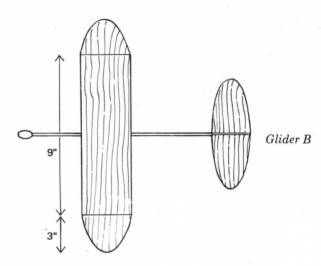

Glider B

9"

3"

The grain of the wood runs from root to tip of flying surfaces, and from nose to tail of fuselage

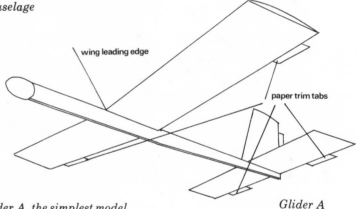

wing leading edge

paper trim tabs

Glider A

above and below *glider B, showing form and filling of wing ribs*

above *glider A, the simplest model for a beginner to make*

The wing of Glider A is simply a piece of 1/32 sheet measuring 8 in × 1½ in. Tailplane and fin are also cut from 1/32 and fuselage from 1/16. This model has dihedral – i.e. the wing tips are raised. Mark centre chord line of the wing, score lightly and run cement along the score mark. Gently crack (not break) the wood. Weight half of the wing down and prop the opposite tip up one inch. When set, cement wing and fuselage in position with leading edge 1/16 inch higher than trailing edge. Hold or prop up while setting, so that wings are correctly lined up. Cement tailplane and fin in place so that they are square-mounted when viewed from the front. Cut ailerons, elevators and rudder from stiff typing paper and cement in place. Add plasticene to nose to bring centre of gravity to the halfway point on the wing chord

below *the Airfix kit of Red Arrows Gnat Trainer*
right *the completed model on its stand*

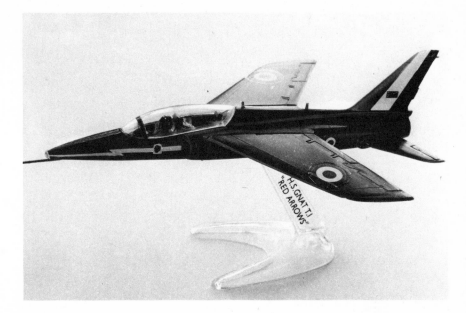

In glider B, opposite, the wing is made in three pieces from 1/32 sheet. Wing ribs cemented to the underside give a curved aerofoil section. Centre section measures 9 in × 3 in. Outboard sections are cut from 3 in squares, wood grain running towards the tip. Wing ribs are all the same shape, two of 1/16 cemented either side of centre chord line, 1/8 inch apart, forming slot for wing mount. Four more ribs from 1/32, are cemented one under each end of centre and inner edge of tip section. Curve wing pieces before cementing. When firm, join wing sections to give 1½ in dihedral under tips. Fuselage takes two pieces of 1/8 sheet. Cement wing mount to fuselage; cement top edge of mount into slot below wing centre chord. Check all square. Tailplane and fin are 1/32 sheet. Add rudder tab of stiff paper; balance model with plasticene

The pictures above show stages in the construction of a 1/72 Red Arrow Gnat Trainer. This is a low price kit and consists of moulded fuselage in two parts, complete with fin, tailplanes, wheels, seats, a transparent cockpit cover and a stand

The Gnat Trainer may be finished with the undercarriage either lowered or retracted. The kit contains very clear instructions for assembly. With any plastic, it is essential to apply the polystyrene cement very sparingly. If surplus cement comes into contact with moulded plastic surfaces other than at the joining edge, the plastic will melt and spoil the appearance. If you decide to paint your model, use the special enamel paints made for this purpose, with good quality brushes. The Gnat in the pictures received a minimum of paintwork. The cockpit interior was painted matt black, the pilot's helmet white and a thin red line was drawn round the base of the cockpit transparency and over the windscreen. Clean brushes in enamel thinners after use, and have a number of brushes of different thicknesses for different tasks

Our next model features a built-up structure from strips of 3/32 inch square balsa strip. Wing ribs and fuselage formers are cut from 1/16 strip. We chose a Keil Kraft Dolphin, a low-price model in the region of £1. The kit is shown on the right. All such kits have easy-to-follow instructions. First cut wing-ribs and other printed parts and put aside. Construction begins with the centre section of the wing.

Lay the plan on the building board. Locate lower spar and trailing edge in position with pins. Note that pins go on either side of strip wood – never through the wood itself.

Cement wing ribs in position. With all joints apply cement to both surfaces and press firmly together. Next the notches at the front of the ribs are filled with cement and the leading edge is pressed into place. Finally the upper spar is added. Outer wing sections and tail surfaces are built up in the same way.

Completed structures are carefully peeled from plan. Outer wing sections are cemented to centre section with the addition of a dihedral brace for extra strength. The wing is then set aside on a flat surface with centre section weighted and tips propped up to give 2½ in of dihedral either side.

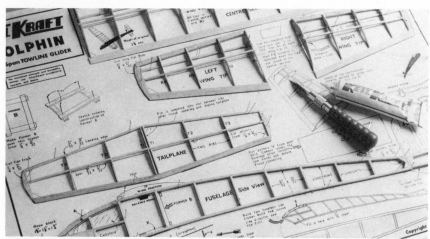

One fuselage side is built on the plan with 3/32 strip held in position with pins. Spacing pieces and cabin roof former are cemented in position. When set a second identical side is built on top of the first. Both sides should be pinned down for two hours.

The fuselage sides are carefully separated with a knife blade and then joined with a sheet balsa former. Upper and lower spacers are added, the structure being held with rubber bands until set.

The finished fuselage and flying surfaces are covered with lightweight tissue attached with tissue paste. Cut tissues slightly oversize and apply paste liberally – especially under wing ribs. On Dolphin, as with many models, the wing is *undercambered* (hollowed). Unless tissue is firmly attached it will pull away from undercamber when shrinking occurs.

After covering leave paste to dry thoroughly. Then spray tissue with an artists mouth spray.

When tissue dries it will shrink to give a drum like surface. Finally the whole model is given a coat of clear dope to protect from moisture.

The completed model should balance at a point one third of chord back from leading edge.

Add lead pellets to weight box in nose block and leave access hole so that weight may be added or removed on flying field.

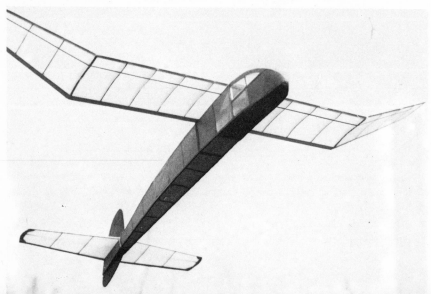

Make your model fly

Glider A (page 66) is intended for flying either indoors or outdoors on a very calm day. Hold slightly nose down with finger and thumb under wing. Push forward gently in a slightly downward path. If the model dives remove a little of the plasticene. If it rises and falls in jerky arcs it is stalling and needs more nose weight. When you have achieved a smooth shallow glide try altering the control surfaces. Left aileron up and right aileron down will turn the model to the left. Left rudder will do the same. Bending the elevators up will cause the model to stall, down elevator will put it in a dive.

With practice this glider can be made to roll and loop. In a ten-foot square room it can be trimmed to consistently circle and return.

Glider B is designed to give a good performance in calm conditions.

From the hand it will circle, loop, or roll off the top of a loop. If trimmed to circle to the left and launched in a steep turn to the right, it will follow a 'figure 8' flight pattern.

Trimming the Dolphin for flight follows the same procedure. Add a rudder tab of stiff paper for turning flight.

Dolphin has towing hooks under the nose. Attach a small curtain ring to a long length of twine and ask a friend to hold the model lightly in a nose-up attitude. Slip the ring over the front hook and tow the model into wind like a kite. The model should climb high into the air. When the tow line is slackened the ring will slip from the hook and Dolphin will be flying free.

Flying models range from simple 'chuck' gliders made of sheet balsa to huge scale models driven by powerful diesel motors and controlled by radio. They can be powered by

Above is a Bristol 1/72 Bulldog from Airfix kit; below, a controlled diesel model under construction

rubber bands, petrol motors, compressed air, electricity and Jetex, an inexpensive form of rocket motor with fuel in pellet form.

69

Fog flying

Fog is cloud which is in contact with the surface of the earth. It presents a serious hazard to movement of any kind. Driving a car in thick fog is an almost impossible task. Even with the most efficient fog lamps the driver may be unable to see the edge of the road. Even walking in fog can be dangerous. The senses are disorientated and it is possible to be hopelessly lost just a hundred yards from home.

You can imagine, therefore, how much more difficult it must be for a pilot to fly in cloud or fog. When walking or driving we can turn only to right or left. An aircraft moves in all three dimensions. In thick fog the pilot's bodily senses cannot tell him for certain if the machine is climbing, diving, rolling, turning or spinning.

Fortunately all modern airliners are equipped with 'blind flying' instruments. The artificial horizon shows whether the aircraft is rolling, diving or climbing. The Turn and Bank Indicator shows degree and accuracy of turn, while the Air Speed Indicator tells the pilot his speed through the air.

Inertial guidance systems tell the pilot his exact position. 'Doppler' navigation equipment indicates speed over the ground plus drift caused by side winds. Other aids can show the aircraft position on a 'rolling' map or 'paint' an ever-changing picture of towns, rivers and coastlines on a cathode ray tube.

With these aids a pilot can fly from any point on the earth's surface to any other point without ever catching a glimpse of the ground. At the end of the journey, however, something more is needed. Ground radar can guide him into line with the runway. Instrument Landing Systems (ILS) will establish him on the correct glide path. But to make a

With the help of new and sophisticated equipment, aircraft can land safely in any visibility

safe visual landing a pilot needs a visibility range of at least 900 metres. If a runway is fogbound a visual landing is impossible and much thought and research has been necessary to overcome this.

The first successful solution to the problem came during the Second World War.

Bombers returning to their bases often found runways wrapped in dense fog. A system of fog dispersal (FIDO) was invented. Pipes carried petrol along the edges of the runway. When landings had to be made in fog, the petrol was ignited. This created so much heat that the fog would be lifted 200–300 feet (60–90m). Pilots would suddenly discover a tunnel of clear air eerily lit by flickering orange flame.

FIDO worked well, but a single runway used up thousands of gallons of petrol in one night. After the war, work began on a system of automatic landing that would work safely in dense fog.

This system is called 'Autoland'. It was first tested in the Hawker Siddeley Trident. It operates in conjunction with the ILS system already installed at all major airports.

Autoland is a robot pilot which flies and lands the aircraft without the pilot touching the controls. For safety, all components are triplicated. If two systems fail the aircraft will still be landed safely by the third, but the odds against all three systems failing are astronomical. Should this happen, the pilot receives ample warning to take control of the aircraft himself and overshoot the runway.

Autoland lines the aircraft up with the runway and establishes it on the correct glide path for touch down. Just above the runway, the throttles close and the control column comes back automatically to 'round out' a moment before touchdown. The Autoland automatic pilot is so successful that there have been occasions when the aircraft has rolled to a stop and the pilot has been unable to taxi to the passenger loading bays because fog has hidden the taxi-ing lights.

In the future even this final stage of the journey will be completed automatically.

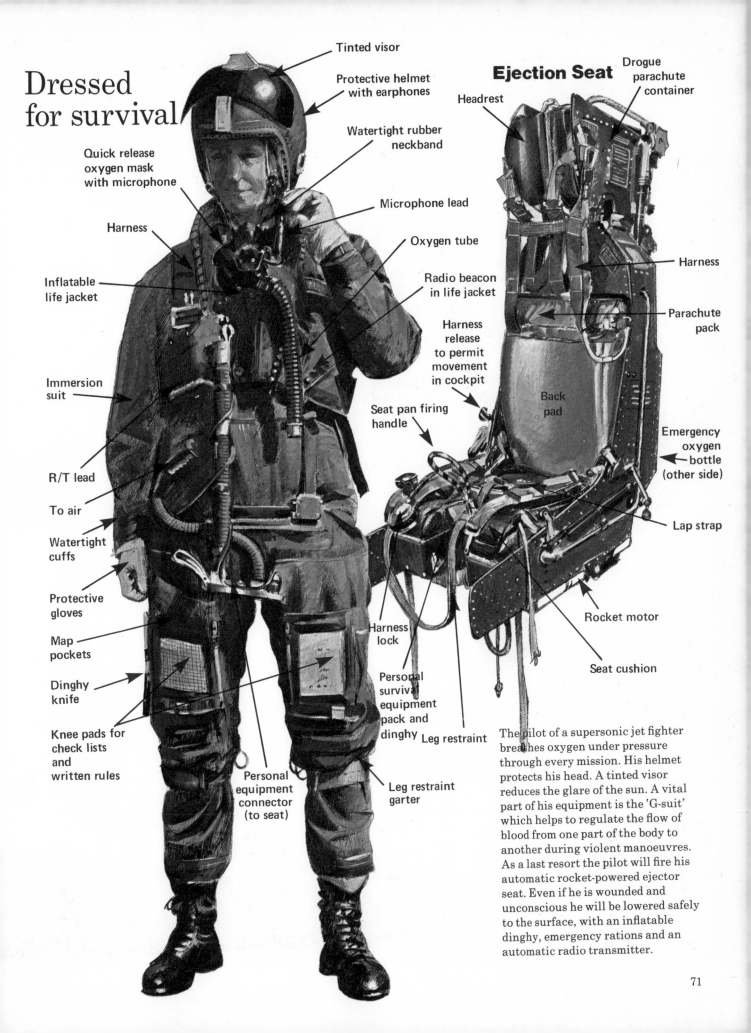

Dressed for survival

Tinted visor

Protective helmet with earphones

Quick release oxygen mask with microphone

Watertight rubber neckband

Microphone lead

Harness

Oxygen tube

Inflatable life jacket

Radio beacon in life jacket

Immersion suit

Harness release to permit movement in cockpit

R/T lead

Seat pan firing handle

To air

Watertight cuffs

Protective gloves

Map pockets

Harness lock

Dinghy knife

Personal survival equipment pack and dinghy

Knee pads for check lists and written rules

Leg restraint

Personal equipment connector (to seat)

Leg restraint garter

Ejection Seat

Drogue parachute container

Headrest

Harness

Parachute pack

Back pad

Emergency oxygen bottle (other side)

Lap strap

Rocket motor

Seat cushion

The pilot of a supersonic jet fighter breathes oxygen under pressure through every mission. His helmet protects his head. A tinted visor reduces the glare of the sun. A vital part of his equipment is the 'G-suit' which helps to regulate the flow of blood from one part of the body to another during violent manoeuvres. As a last resort the pilot will fire his automatic rocket-powered ejector seat. Even if he is wounded and unconscious he will be lowered safely to the surface, with an inflatable dinghy, emergency rations and an automatic radio transmitter.

Trainers

Tiger, the immortal de Havilland DH 82 Tiger Moth, was the most famous trainer of them all.

The men who flew the Spitfires and Hurricanes in the Battle of Britain learned their trade in the back cockpit of a Tiger Moth. So too did pilots of many other countries: America, Canada, New Zealand, Australia, India, Sweden, Norway, Denmark, Portugal....

It was said that a pilot who mastered a Tiger could fly anything on wings. Certainly this dainty little biplane broke the heart of many a novice, but those who gained their wings on de Havilland's masterpiece remember her with all the affection of a first love.

The very first Tiger of them all took the air at Stag Lane on 22 October 1931. When production ended in 1945 more than 8,800 had been built. Today, almost fifty years after that memorable first flight, Tigers are still to be seen at flying club airfields around the world, and new pilots are still proud to say: 'I learned to fly on a Tiger Moth!'

Hawk. The Hawker Siddeley HS 1182 Hawk belongs to the new generation of Royal Air Force aeroplanes. Together with the Jaguar and the Panavia MRCA, it will carry RAF pilots through the closing years of the twentieth century and into the world of 2001.

Initially the Hawk will replace the RAF's ageing Gnat and Hunter Trainers in the advanced training and weapons training roles. Later it will also take over the basic jet

Bulldog is a basic military trainer in service with the air forces of six countries. Built by Scottish Aviation of Prestwick, it is fully aerobatic. Instructor and pupil sit side by side in a spacious cockpit with magnificent all-round visibility, and there is a third seat in the rear of the aircraft.

Power is provided by a 200hp Lycoming engine. The top speed is 150mph (240km/h) and the Bulldog can climb to its aerobatic training height of 1,500m in six minutes. The Bulldog is a more powerful development of the Beagle Pup civil aircraft, and when the Beagle Aircraft Company went out of business in 1970 the design was taken over by Scottish Aviation of Prestwick.

training role now filled by the Jet Provost T. Mark V.

When that time comes, RAF pilots will be able to complete their entire jet training course on a single aircraft type. Obviously this will save money, since fewer aircraft will be needed to train pilots. It will not be necessary either to hold as many airframe and engine spares in store, and the training courses for maintenance engineers and mechanics can be greatly simplified.

Further savings in cost will come from the fact that the Hawk is powered by the Rolls-Royce Turbomeca Adour turbofan – the same basic engine that powers the Jaguar motorcar.

One hundred and seventy-five Hawks are on order for the Royal Air Force and many more orders are expected from abroad. The combination of a low-cost 'three in one' training aircraft with a potent ground attack capability is one that seems certain to appeal to the air forces of many countries.

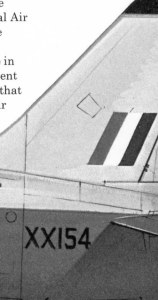

From piston engine to fan-jet

Rolls-Royce Merlin piston engine

Rolls-Royce RB211 fan jet engine

For centuries man knew the basic requirements of heavier-than-air flight. What he lacked was a lightweight source of power to enable him to turn theory into practice.

The Wright brothers recognized the problem. When they had perfected their third glider, they designed and built a light but powerful motor fuelled with gasolene. That tiny motor was the prototype for many hundreds of thousands of piston-driven aero engines ranging from the 12hp engine of the Wright Flyer to the mighty 3,800hp motors which powered the vast B-36 bomber.

The piston aero engine reigned supreme for almost fifty years. By the beginning of the Second World War, however, it was clear that the use of a piston engine to turn a conventional propeller was becoming outdated.

Various alternatives were tried. Messerschmitt built the spectacular Me163 liquid-fuel rocket fighter which flew at 600mph (960km/h) and could climb to over 15,000 metres. However, it used so much fuel that operational endurance could be measured in minutes.

Another kind of engine to be investigated was the 'pulse jet' which powered the V-1 flying bomb. This worked reasonably well, but also used too much fuel. 'Ram jets' were tried by German and French designers. These consisted of an open tube with a venturi (egg-timer

shaped) interior. It had no moving parts and could deliver very high power, but it had one big disadvantage. A ram jet cannot be started until it is moving at more than 200mph (320km/h). This meant that a ram-jet powered aircraft had to be launched with another type of power plant to enable it to reach the minimum 'lighting-up' speed.

In Italy, the Caproni aircraft company almost solved the problem with a 'ducted fan' propulsion unit. This was a propeller mounted inside a large-diameter tube and powered by a piston engine. The designer of the power plant was named Campini, and the aircraft in which it flew was designated Caproni/Campini CC1.

The CC1 looked like a modern single-jet machine. It flew in 1940, but its success was limited.

Two men, working independently and unaware of each other's research, were to create the successor to the piston-driven aero engine. They were Hans-Joachim Pabst von Ohain in Germany and Frank Whittle in Britain. The first Whittle gas turbine ran successfully on a test rig in April 1937. Later in the same year von Ohain demonstrated his HeS 2A turbine.

Ernst Heinkel, the famous German aircraft designer, recognized the possibilities of jet propulsion. He had given his support to von Ohain's

research and now began to build the world's first true jet-propelled aircraft. The Heinkel He178V1 made a satisfactory first flight on 27 August 1939, and without official backing Heinkel pressed ahead with the design of a twin jet fighter designated He280.

The He280V1 flew on 2 April 1941. It was the most revolutionary aeroplane ever to fly, and the greatest step forward since the Wright Flyer. Powered by two HeS8A centrifugal turbojets, it had a fully retractable nose-wheel undercarriage and a compressed-air ejection seat for the pilot. Fully loaded the He280V1 had a maximum speed of 485mph (776km/h), and later versions were expected to reach speeds of more than 550mph (880km/h). Incredibly the world's most advanced aeroplane was not ordered into production.

Meanwhile, in Britain, a similar lack of official interest delayed the first flight of the Gloster Whittle E28/39 jet aircraft until May 1941. This machine, which is now on display at the Science Museum in London, had a speed of 300mph (480km/h), thanks to the power of the first Whittle W.1. centrifugal turbojet. Later, after it was fitted with a more powerful motor, the E28/39 reached a speed of 466mph (744km/h) and climbed to a height of

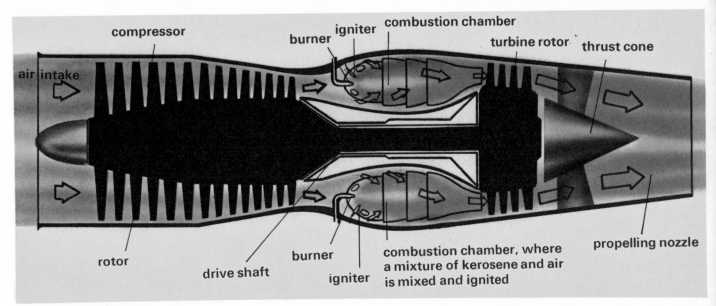

compressor   igniter   combustion chamber

air intake   burner   turbine rotor   thrust cone

rotor   burner   combustion chamber, where a mixture of kerosene and air is mixed and ignited

drive shaft   igniter

propelling nozzle

Axial-flow turbojet

12,800 metres. Air Ministry and RAF test pilots were soon convinced that the jet was the power plant of the future, and the Gloster Aircraft Company was ordered to carry on with the design of a twin-jet fighter to be named Meteor.

In Germany Professor Willy Messerschmitt has also recognized the great potential of jet propulsion. In 1938 he began design work on a twin-jet fighter which was designated Me262. Construction of three Me262 prototypes began in 1940. The first of these, Me262V1, flew in April 1941 powered only by a piston engine mounted in the nose. In March 1942 its power was increased by the addition of two BMW turbojets, but both jets failed on the test flight and the pilot narrowly avoided a crash.

The third prototype, Me262V3, was fitted with Jumo turbojets and it flew successfully on 18 July 1942. A month later, after several satisfactory test flights, the machine was flown by an Air Ministry test pilot. This most important trial was not a success. As a result of pilot error, caused by inexperience of the aircraft's revolutionary power plants and the way the plane would behave, the Me262V3 failed to take off.

The German Air Ministry already had some doubts about the value of jet propulsion, and this incident did nothing for the reputation of the new fighter. Although later prototypes performed brilliantly, easily

exceeding 500mph (800km/h) in level flight, Air Ministry officials continued to show little interest in the aircraft for many months.

Eventually, the value of the Messerschmitt fighter was recognized and the order was given to put it into production.

The Me262 heralded the opening of the jet age. After its appearance, development of the turbojet engine was rapid. The Gloster Meteor fighter went into service with the RAF and a Whittle gas turbine was sent to the United States to power the Bell Aerocomet fighter. With this the American jet industry was born. By September 1948 the de Havilland 108 research aircraft had exceeded the speed of sound, and in May 1952 the de Havilland Comet, the world's first jetliner, went into service with BOAC.

Turbojet-powered airliners became bigger and more powerful. More power meant more noise at take-off and landing. People living close to international airports banded together to protest, and a new term 'noise pollution' entered the English language.

For a while it was thought that the propeller-turbine – a jet engine driving a propeller – would provide the answer to quieter flight. However, the prop-jet's maximum speed was only about 500mph (800km/h). As a result, prop-jet airliners such as the Viscount, Vanguard, Electra and Britannia enjoyed only a brief success. Air

passengers, however, certainly wanted higher speeds and shorter journey times. They showed this by booking their flights on the faster but noisier turbojetliners.

The problem, therefore, which faced the aero-engine designers was to develop an engine which would be less noisy, more powerful and able to fly faster.

The answer lay in the ducted fan which had been tried experimentally on the Caproni/Campini CC1 in 1940. Now the plan was to drive a ducted fan by means of a powerful jet motor. The hot gases of the jet exhaust were shrouded in the mass of cold air pushed back by the fan, blanketing the noise of the engine. Apart from being much quieter than ordinary jet engines, turbofans proved to be much more efficient; they provided more power but used less fuel.

Big turbofans delivering a thrust of over 18,000kg were built to provide the power for the Boeing 747, the first 'Jumbo' jet. A single 747 can carry 400 passengers. That equals the passenger capacity of three or four smaller airliners.

Not only are the 'Jumbos' quieter than their smaller counterparts, but fewer landings and take-offs are needed to carry the same number of passengers. This, in turn, means still less noise and explains why the Jumbos are popular not only with their passengers, but also with the people who live beneath their flight paths or close to large airports.

Beaufighter

When the Battle of Britain ended in September 1940 the 'blitz' began. Every night air-raid sirens would drive millions of people from their beds to huddle in cold, damp shelters. In London, underground stations were crowded with families trying to snatch a few hours sleep. Luftwaffe bombers roamed the night sky unopposed. The Spitfire, with its narrow track undercarriage, was dangerous to land in the dark. The Hurricane could fly at night, but its pilots had no means of finding the enemy.

The first hope of a change in the RAF's fortune came with the radar-equipped Blenheim Mk.1. Unfortunately the Blenheim was only very slightly faster than the He 111, and slower than a Ju 88. The battle was still a one-sided contest. On 14 November 1940, 400 Luftwaffe bombers destroyed the centre of Coventry. As the city burned, the RAF launched more than a hundred night fighters against the bomber stream, but not a single enemy plane was destroyed.

Then the Beaufighter entered the battle. Two 1,500hp Hercules engines gave this massive fighter a speed of 320mph (512km/h). Its terrifying armament of four cannons and six machine guns could tear an enemy bomber apart. Even more important, the Beaufighter carried AI Mk.IV – airborne interception radar.

At last, night fighter crews could see in the dark. On the night of 19 November 1940 Sgt. J. Phillipson crouched over his screen in the back seat of a 'Beau'. A blip of light showed the track of a 'bandit'. He called directions to his pilot, Flt. Lt. John Cunningham, and the Beaufighter stalked her prey through the black velvet sky.

'You're right behind him, Skipper.' Ahead, Cunningham saw the flicker of twin exhausts in the darkness.

'I see him.' Stealthily the Beaufighter overtook the raider. Then the pilot's searching eyes made out the silhouette of a Ju 88 intensely black against the starry background.

Four streams of fire leapt from the Beaufighter's nose. Brilliant flashes sparkled against the bomber's wing and engine nacelle, or outer casing.

An engine began to burn. First just a tiny trickle of flame, then a torrent of fire as the stricken aircraft rolled slowly onto her back and plunged towards the earth far below.

Radar was top secret in 1940. To explain the victory an RAF press officer told reporters that the pilot ate carrots to help him see in the dark. Since that night John Cunningham has been known as 'Cat's Eye'.

The engagement showed what could be achieved with radar-equipped night fighters. More and more Beaufighters flowed from the factories. More and more German bombers failed to return from missions over England.

On 19 May 1941, just six months after the catastrophic Coventry raid, the Luftwaffe made a massive assault on London. This time Beaufighters were patrolling the approaches to the target. The night sky echoed to the crackle of cannon fire. Again and again plunging fireballs marked the last moments of a falling raider. Twenty-four bombers failed to return to their bases in France that night, and the Luftwaffe never returned to Britain in strength.

Nimrod

'...RAF Nimrods are searching for a Hull trawler which was last reported 150 miles (240km) south west of Iceland...'

Nimrods are often in the news, searching for a missing ship, watching over a crippled tanker, or hunting a solo yachtsman whose radio has failed. However, some of the other duties performed by these graceful grey/white monsters are less widely reported. When Russian warships sail up the English Channel a Nimrod will be around to maintain a discreet watch. Smugglers too have learned respect for Nimrod's tireless electronic eyes, whether their cargo is illegal immigrants or guns for the IRA.

The Hawker Siddeley Nimrod is descended directly from the Comet jetliner. Her famous ancestry shows in every line. The first two 'pre-production' Nimrods were converted from Comet Mk.IV airframes, and engine bays were enlarged to accommodate Spey turbofans in place of the old Avon turbojets.

With the new engines Nimrod has an endurance of more than twelve hours. It can fly to its search area at 550mph (880km/h). Then, by shutting down two motors, it can cruise at low speed for the duration of the patrol, accelerating to 550mph (880km/h) for the return to base.

The very strong airframe inherited from the Comet gives Nimrod an unrivalled ability to operate in the turbulent air close to the water. In fact RAF Nimrods operate so close to the waves that each machine has to have the salt spray washed off with high pressure hoses as soon as it returns to base.

The most obvious difference between Nimrod and Comet is the huge weapons bay beneath the fuselage. Here is stored the arsenal of anti-submarine missiles. The fuselage above it is packed with electronic surveillance equipment.

Above the waves, Nimrod's electronic feelers search out and identify any object from a submarine periscope to a nuclear-powered aircraft carrier. Below the surface sonar buoys, dropped in a carefully charted pattern, track and report every moving object.

Nimrod has another potent search weapon called MAD – the Magnetic Anomaly Detector – which can measure tiny variations in the Earth's magnetic field. Such variations may be natural, or they may indicate a nuclear submarine hiding in the depths.

opposite: *the Beaufighter in action*
left: *Nimrod shadows the Soviet Navy helicopter carrier* Leningrad
below: *the flight deck of a Nimrod*
bottom: *Nimrod on an exercise with Royal Navy submarines*

Aerobatics

Instructors from the Central Flying School perform close formation aerobatics at Farnborough. The yellow aircraft are Hawker-Siddeley Gnats accompanied by Jet Provosts of the Red Pelican aerobatic team
left: Hawker-Siddeley Jaguars ground-attack aircraft in close formation

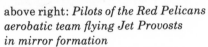

above right: *Pilots of the Red Pelicans aerobatic team flying Jet Provosts in mirror formation*

right: *Red Arrows in 'diamond nine' formation*

below: *Red Pelicans trailing smoke as they pull out of a loop*

Tomcat

Grumman's F-14 Tomcat is aptly named. This two-seat naval fighter is one of the deadliest fighting machines ever built. At take-off Tomcat may weigh more than 31,000kgm – four tons more than a fully loaded B-17 Flying Fortress in the Second World War. Her maximum war-load, consisting of air-to-air and air-to-ground missiles plus bombs and cannon shells, weighs 6,591kg. That is more than the total bomb loads of three Flying Fortresses.

And yet this extraordinary warplane can take off and land on the deck of an aircraft carrier. Boosted by twin 13,000kg-thrust turbofans with afterburners, F-14 can climb like a rocket to 21,000m and accelerate to 1,700mph (2,720km/h), or two-and-a-half times the speed of sound. At the other end of the speed scale the Tomcat can fly safely at speeds as low as 120mph (192km/h).

In a dog-fight Tomcat can outmanoeuvre any adversary. At high sub-sonic speeds, that is up to about 750mph (1,200km/h), it can turn so tightly that the crew are subjected to 'G' forces in excess of eight times the force of gravity. To survive such enormous pressures crewmen wear G-suits. These control the flow of blood around the body and help to prevent 'blacking out' – a loss of vision caused by blood draining away from the head.

The secret of the Tomcat's performance lies in the 'swing wing'.

The swing wing, sometimes called variable geometry (VG), allows the pilot to change the shape of his aircraft in flight. For low-speed flying the wing swings forward. This gives a very efficient lifting surface equipped with high-lift devices on leading and trailing edges. At very high speeds the wing is swept back 60° to give a dart-like or *delta* plan form.

Most aerial combat takes place at speeds up to and just above the speed of sound. For this the wing is swept to an intermediate position. Very powerful air-brakes allow the pilot to decelerate rapidly and special manoeuvring flaps reduce the radius of the turning circle, enabling Tomcat to 'turn inside' any opponent.

The ideal degree of sweepback varies for every condition of flight, depending on air-speed, altitude, G-force and all-up-weight. In normal flight the pilot selects the wing position. In combat, however, airspeed, altitude and turning radius vary constantly. Each change requires a different wing setting for peak performance. Such calculations are beyond the capabilities of any human pilot engaged in life or death combat.

In these circumstances the pilot switches in the *Mach Sweep Programmer*. MSP is a computer which handles both wing sweep and manoeuvring flaps, leaving the pilot free to concentrate on his opponent.

Another computer programmes and controls the Phoenix and Sidewinder missiles which are Tomcat's main offensive armament. The Hughes AWG-9 weapon control system locates and identifies hostile aircraft by means of radar and infra-red heat seeking sensors. When weapon control has locked onto a target within a five-mile radius the pilot can launch a missile without even having to point his aircraft at the target. If necessary the computer can lock on and engage up to six widely separated targets simultaneously.

Tomcat aircrews practise interceptions against radio-controlled target drones. Sometimes the drones come in at

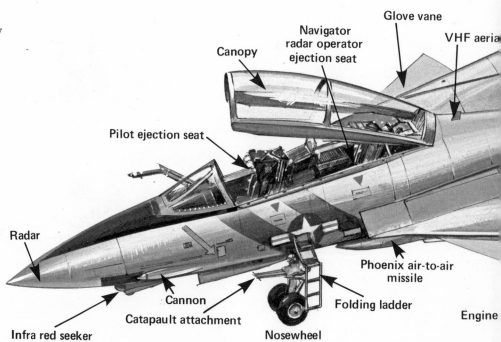

Glove vane

Navigator radar operator ejection seat

VHF aeria

Canopy

Pilot ejection seat

Radar

Phoenix air-to-air missile

Cannon

Catapult attachment

Folding ladder

Infra red seeker

Nosewheel

Engine

2,000mph (3,200km/h) at a height of 24,000m above the surface. Others skim the waves at the speed of sound. So far, both types have been met and destroyed in impressive demonstrations of the Tomcat's firepower.

More than 500 Grumman Tomcats are on order for the US Navy and the US Marines. The first squadrons are already at sea aboard the giant carrier USS *Enterprise*. Now many other navies and air forces are thinking about buying this most versatile warplane.

Variable geometry – the shape of the future. Grumman's F14 Tomcat fighter for the United States Navy can fly at 1,700mph – 2.5 times the speed of sound

GRUMMAN F-14 TOMCAT

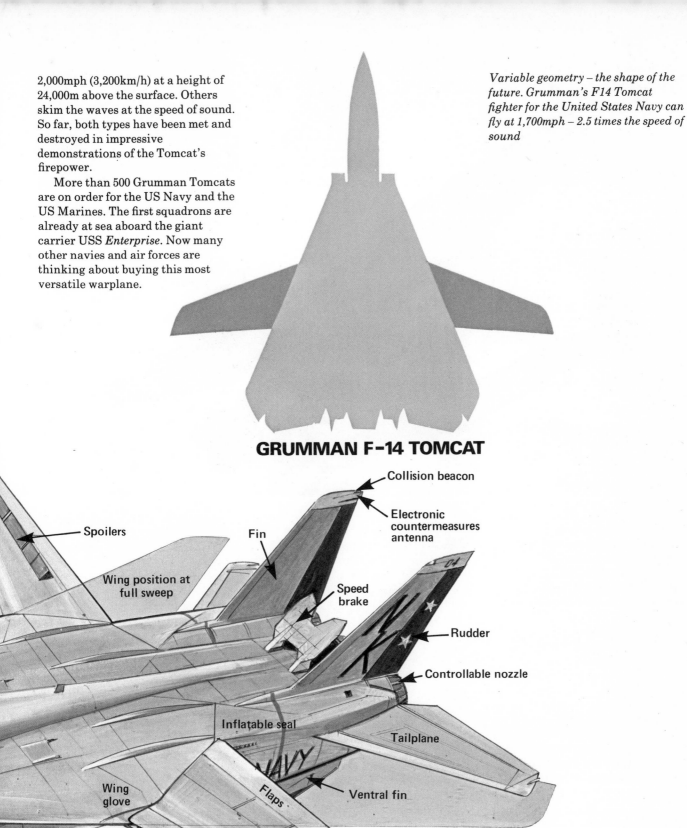

Collision beacon

Electronic countermeasures antenna

Spoilers

Fin

Wing position at full sweep

Speed brake

Rudder

Controllable nozzle

Inflatable seal

Tailplane

Wing glove

Flaps

Ventral fin

Phoenix AAM

Mainwheel

Wing leading edge slat

Formation lights

Intake

Strange shapes in the sky

The Westland-Delanne Lysander with a 4-gun turret above the rear wing

During the Second World War both sides were constantly trying to outdo their opponents in the air. Strange and novel ideas were explored by aircraft designers. As a result many unusual and sometimes bizarre shapes were to be seen in the skies over Europe. Let us take a look at three such experiments which each came very close to success.

The Westland-Delanne Lysander was born in the desperate days of 1940. This plane was a tandem wing (one wing behind the other) adaptation of a standard army co-operation aircraft. The plan was to mount a four-gun Boulton Paul turret on the well-tried and tested Lysander airframe. It was one of many unorthodox weapons devised to combat the expected German invasion. In action the Delanne Lysander would have flown low over the invasion beaches, pouring a devastating hail of fire into enemy landing barges.

In order to balance the considerable weight of the gun turret, Westland's experts adopted an aerodynamic layout that had been pioneered in France by M. Delanne. The standard Lysander tail unit was removed and replaced with a second wing. This second wing provided a considerable proportion of the aircraft's total lift and allowed the designer to shift the aeroplane's centre of gravity to the rear.

Despite the unusual layout, Westland test pilot Harold Penrose was delighted with the performance and handling characteristics of the Delanne Lysander. By the time the flight test programme had been completed, however, the threat of invasion had receded and this most unusual warplane was consigned to the scrap heap.

The Miles Aircraft Company also experimented with tandem wing designs. The brothers Miles planned a naval fighter with the pilot seated in the extreme nose. This would have given him a magnificent view both for combat and for the hazardous task of landing on the pitching deck of an aircraft carrier. The engine was to be mounted at the rear, driving a pusher propeller, with weapons and ammunition stored amidships.

The tandem wing was the only layout which allowed the weight to be distributed in this way. It also resulted in a compact airframe which would fit more easily into the narrow confines of an aircraft-carrier hangar.

In order to test their ideas, the Miles brothers built a small flying test rig. Named the Miles M35 Libellula (dragonfly), it was first flown by George Miles on 1 May 1942. The M35 was not a great success, and no order was given for the further development of this naval fighter. The experiment, however, did provide valuable information about the flying characteristics of tandem wing aircraft.

Later, when the Air Ministry issued a specification for a high speed day bomber, the Miles Aircraft Company designed a new tandem wing aeroplane based on the lessons learned from the M35. Numbered M39 and again bearing the name Libellula, it was to be powered by twin Rolls-Royce Merlin engines. Once again, to prove their design the Miles brothers built the piloted scale model illustrated above. It was numbered M39B and was 5/8 of the size of the proposed bomber. Power was provided by twin de Havilland

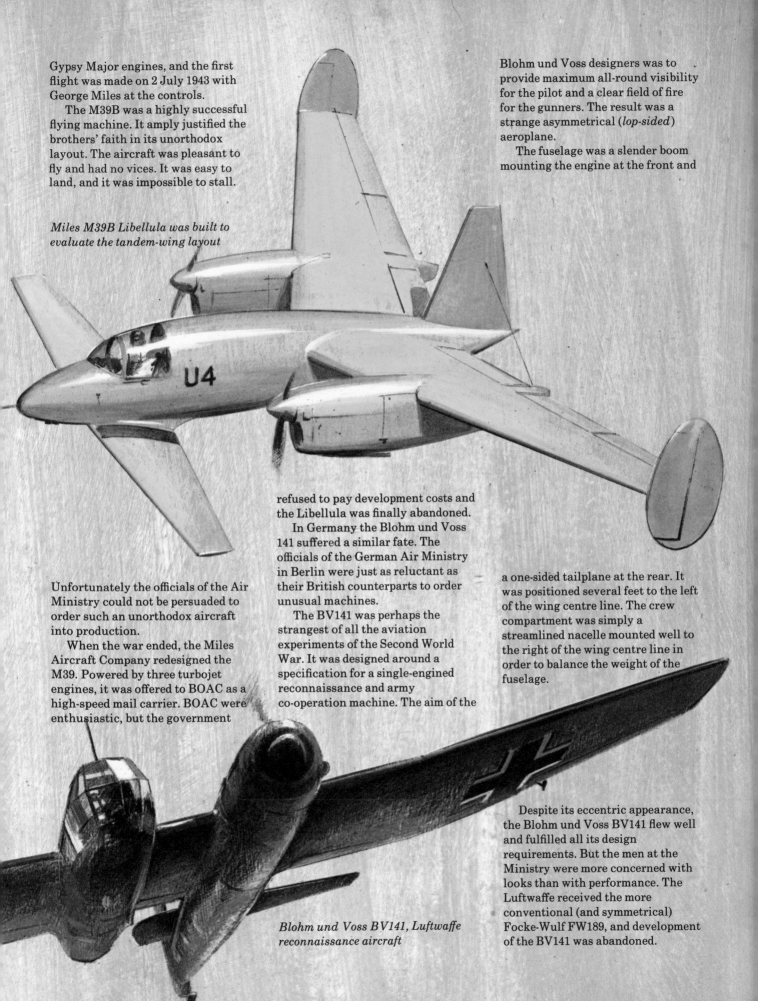

Gypsy Major engines, and the first flight was made on 2 July 1943 with George Miles at the controls.

The M39B was a highly successful flying machine. It amply justified the brothers' faith in its unorthodox layout. The aircraft was pleasant to fly and had no vices. It was easy to land, and it was impossible to stall.

Miles M39B Libellula was built to evaluate the tandem-wing layout

Unfortunately the officials of the Air Ministry could not be persuaded to order such an unorthodox aircraft into production.

When the war ended, the Miles Aircraft Company redesigned the M39. Powered by three turbojet engines, it was offered to BOAC as a high-speed mail carrier. BOAC were enthusiastic, but the government refused to pay development costs and the Libellula was finally abandoned.

In Germany the Blohm und Voss 141 suffered a similar fate. The officials of the German Air Ministry in Berlin were just as reluctant as their British counterparts to order unusual machines.

The BV141 was perhaps the strangest of all the aviation experiments of the Second World War. It was designed around a specification for a single-engined reconnaissance and army co-operation machine. The aim of the Blohm und Voss designers was to provide maximum all-round visibility for the pilot and a clear field of fire for the gunners. The result was a strange asymmetrical (*lop-sided*) aeroplane.

The fuselage was a slender boom mounting the engine at the front and a one-sided tailplane at the rear. It was positioned several feet to the left of the wing centre line. The crew compartment was simply a streamlined nacelle mounted well to the right of the wing centre line in order to balance the weight of the fuselage.

Blohm und Voss BV141, Luftwaffe reconnaissance aircraft

Despite its eccentric appearance, the Blohm und Voss BV141 flew well and fulfilled all its design requirements. But the men at the Ministry were more concerned with looks than with performance. The Luftwaffe received the more conventional (and symmetrical) Focke-Wulf FW189, and development of the BV141 was abandoned.

Great war planes

*Gloster Gladiator, the only biplane
fighter of the Second World War*

*Curtiss P-40 Warhawk in the colours
of the Chinese Air Force*

*Junkers Ju 87B, the divebomber that
spearheaded Hitler's blitzkrieg*

Stuka. With its angular cranked
wing and great spatted wheels
reaching forward like the talons of
some monstrous hawk, Junker's
Ju 87B was a sight to strike fear into
the bravest heart. Its noise was still
more terrifying. To the harsh roar of
the Jumo engine was added the
banshee wail of wind-driven sirens.
Then would come the rising scream of
a falling bomb.

Massed formations of Stukas
spearheaded Hitler's 'blitzkrieg' in
the spring of 1940 and played a major
role in the defeat of the British and

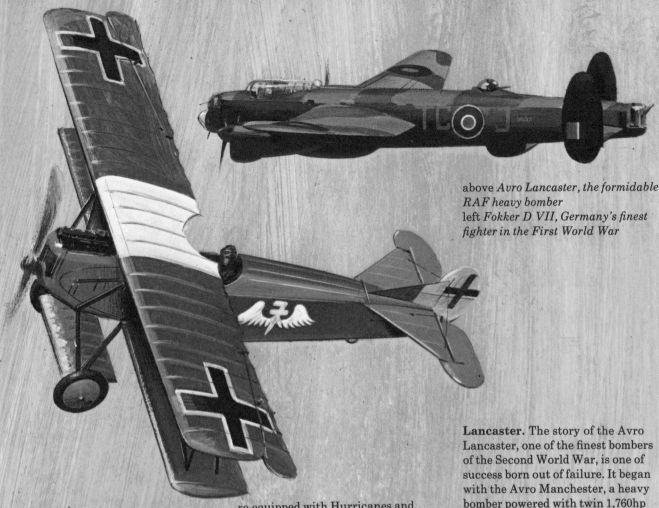

above *Avro Lancaster, the formidable RAF heavy bomber*
left *Fokker D VII, Germany's finest fighter in the First World War*

French armies. The Stuka met its match over the beaches of Dunkirk, however, suffering very heavy losses at the hands of British fighter pilots. Casualties mounted still further in the ensuing Battle of Britain. By August 1940 the Ju 87B had been withdrawn from front line service.

Warhawk. The Curtiss P-40 served in every theatre of war and flew the colours of many nations. In various marks it was named *Tomahawk*, *Kittyhawk* and *Warhawk*. The P-40 first saw action against Japanese bombers over China. Flown by American volunteer pilots of the famous Tiger Squadron, these machines sported the fearsome sharkstooth insignia that was later to become the P-40's trademark throughout the Mediterranean war zone and across the Pacific from Darwin to the Aleutians.

Gladiator. The Gloster Gladiator was the last biplane fighter to serve with the RAF. When war came in 1939 it was already obsolete, and front line squadrons had long since re-equipped with Hurricanes and Spitfires. Despite this, Gladiators saw service in Norway, in defence of Plymouth during the Battle of Britain, and in the Middle East. It was over the Mediterranean that the Gladiator won its greatest battle honours. Flt. Lt. M. T. St. J. Pattle, D.F.C., the RAF's top-scoring fighter ace, destroyed at least twenty-four enemy aircraft while flying his Gladiator from bases in Greece.

Fokker D VII. Anthony Fokker's sleek D VII biplane was probably the best fighter of the First World War. Highly manoeuvrable at all altitudes, it had a maximum speed of 125mph (200km/h) and could climb to 3,000km in just over eight minutes. The first D VIIs were delivered to the Luftwaffe in the spring of 1918. Within six months almost all German fighter formations had re-equipped with the new fighter. The most famous of these units was the Richthofen Jagdgeschwader commanded by Oberleutnant Hermann Goering, later to command the Luftwaffe in the Second World War.

Lancaster. The story of the Avro Lancaster, one of the finest bombers of the Second World War, is one of success born out of failure. It began with the Avro Manchester, a heavy bomber powered with twin 1,760hp Rolls-Royce Vulture engines. From the beginning the Manchester was plagued by engine and propeller failures, and after eighteen months the type was withdrawn from service.

To overcome the problems of the Vulture, a Mark III version of the Manchester was designed to be powered by four Rolls-Royce Merlin engines. The combination of Manchester airframe with the tried and tested Merlins proved highly successful. The new machine, renamed Lancaster, was ordered into mass production. To speed its entry into service many partly completed Manchesters were converted to Lancaster standard.

In all, 7,377 Lancasters were built in Britain and Canada. The type flew more than 150,000 sorties and dropped over 600,000 tons of bombs. The most famous Lancaster of them all, R5868 or S for Sugar, can be seen today in the RAF Museum at Hendon. On her side are painted bomb symbols representing 137 operational sorties, together with Goering's boast that 'No enemy plane will fly over Reich territory.'

Designs of today and tomorrow

above: *F-15 Eagle, maximum Mach No. 2.5, in service with the USAF*

Here we see some of the aeroplanes that will shape the future of aviation in the next quarter of a century. They are built for a long life and we may be sure that many of them will still be flying at the beginning of the Twenty First Century.

We can be equally certain that the year 2001 will show fantastic machines with performances beyond our imaginings. What would a schoolboy of 1950 have thought of the Harrier lifting vertically from a forest clearing and streaking away at the speed of sound? Or of a fighter like Eagle which weighs more than a Flying Fortress heavy bomber and yet can climb vertically at supersonic speed? Or of the Lockheed Blackbird which can 'beat the sun' across the Atlantic and land in America several

hours before it took off from Britain?

Just what might the future hold for aviation in the year 2001? We have some clues in the research being carried out today. Almost certainly man will develop new sources of power to replace failing supplies of oil. We may see a 5,000mph jetliner carrying 500 passengers and powered by engines burning liquid hydrogen. The hydrogen would be deprived from seawater. When burnt in the atmosphere it would produce an exhaust of nothing more toxic than water – and that in time would return to the sea.

Already a hydrogen fuelled car is running on American roads, and the air-liner described above is taking shape on the drawing boards of the McDonnell Douglas Company.

Another source of power might be derived from nuclear fission or fusion. Nuclear power could turn ducted fans to drive the 600 feet span aerial tankers and bulk carriers now in the planning stage. Nuclear engines could also power vast mile-long airships filled with helium gas. Such vessels would have almost unlimited range. They could remain airborne for a year or more at a time, passengers and cargo being loaded and unloaded by 'flying crane'

helicopters.

Further in the future lies an even more exciting possibility. Scientists in many countries are investigating the nature of gravity and the effects of electro-gravetic forces. In London's Imperial College there is a 1/6 scale vehicle which can float several inches above its track supported by an invisible force field.

One day man may discover the means of controlling and reversing the force of gravity. Such a discovery would revolutionise not only aerial transport, but every aspect of human locomotion from climbing the stairs to crossing the solar system.

left *the Sea Harrier, a fighter plane designed for use on the Royal Navy's through-deck cruisers*

top *General Dynamics F-16 lightweight air superiority fighter*
below *Short SD3-30 STOL 'feeder-liner'*

Quiz

1   Name the manufacturer and service designation of the famous Flying Fortress
2   Name the RAF's first jet bomber and its designation in the United States Air Force
3   What were the unusual features of the de Havilland Sea Vixen?
4   What is the meaning of the term 'delta wing'?
5   What do the letters MRCA stand for?
6   Ancestors of the MRCA fought on opposite sides in the Battle of Britain. Do you know what aircraft these were?
7   What is a 'hush kit'?
8   Name two ten-engined aeroplanes
9   What was the unusual feature of power plant of the B-36s?
10 Name the biggest warplane of the Second World War
11 Who commanded RAF Fighter Command in the Battle of Britain?
12 Who was in charge of the Luftwaffe in the Battle of Britain?
13 Name the aircraft type which sank four Japanese aircraft carriers in the Battle of Midway
14 Name the world's first all-metal passenger aircraft
15 In what year did the Wright brothers make the world's first powered flight?
16 Who was Otto Lilienthal?
17 Which of the two Wright brothers made the first powered flight?
18 Who has been called the true inventor of the aeroplane? Why?
19 How does a glider pilot keep his machine in the air for long periods?
20 What is the difference between thermalling and slope soaring?
21 What is the difference between cumulus and cumulo-nimbus clouds?
22 Name two methods by which gliders are launched
23 How could you distinguish between a Boeing 707 and a Boeing 747 'Jumbo' jet?
24 What is the purpose of the Canadair CL-215 water bomber?
25 What unusual feature was shared by the D.H. Albatross and the D.H. Mosquito?
26 What is the purpose of the Lockheed SR-71A 'Blackbird'?
27 Hendon was famous for spectacular air displays. What is Hendon famous for today?
28 Who was the designer of the Hurricane, Typhoon, Tempest and Harrier?
29 What is the Shuttleworth Trust?
30 Name the type of aircraft which carried 5,577 passengers without injury in the four years before the First World War?
31 In the Science Museum in London you can see a famous aeroplane named 'Jason'. Why is this machine and its pilot a part of aviation history?
32 What happened at 16.23 Eastern Daylight Time on Sunday, 20 July 1969?
33 What do the letters V.T.O.L. stand for?
34 Name the first V.T.O.L. aircraft to enter service
35 The Grumman Tomcat is a variable-geometry aircraft. Can you explain what is meant by 'variable-geometry'?
36 Why do most helicopters have a tail rotor?
37 Name the first practicable helicopter
38 What is the meaning of the abbreviation S.T.O.L.?
39 What is a mock-up in aviation language?
40 Why is M. Jacques Schneider remembered in aviation history?
41 Explain the effect of the elevator on an aeroplane's flight
42 What is Autoland?
43 Name the most widely used British training aircraft of the Second World War
44 Who designed and built the world's first gasoline-fuelled aero engine?
45 Who demonstrated the world's first aero gas turbine (jet) engine?
46 Name the first successful jet powered aircraft
47 Which was the first jet powered aeroplane to enter military service?
48 Who built the world's first jetliner? What is it called?
49 What is a fan-jet?
50 Name the famous German dive bomber of 1940. What were its chief recognition features?

Glossary

Aerofoil: a body (wing, tailplane etc.) producing aerodynamic force by movement through air

Aileron: moveable control surface, usually on trailing edge of wing

Airbrake: device to increase drag and thus reduce or limit airspeed

Airflow: air movement over surface

Airframe: structure of aircraft excluding power unit

Airscrew: systems of aerofoils rotating around axis to convert engine power into thrust

Airship: navigable lighter-than-air craft raised by helium or hydrogen

Air speed indicator (ASI): instrument registering speed of aircraft in relation to surrounding air

Angle of attack: angle at which an aerofoil meets the airflow

Angle of incidence: angle of aerofoil in relation to datum line of fuselage

Artificial horizon: instrument to register position of aircraft in relation to true horizon

Autogiro: see Gyrocopter

Axial flow turbojet: gas turbine with series of compressor blades mounted one behind the other

Bank: degree of tilt of an aeroplane wing to the horizontal

Barograph: recording barometer in sailplane to record altitude/time

Camber: convex shape of upper wing surface; undercamber: concave shape of under surface

Centre of gravity: point at which aircraft balances if suspended

Centrifugal flow turbojet: gas turbine aero engine in which air is compressed by being flung outwards by blades mounted on revolving circular plate

Cockpit: aircrew compartment

Control column (joystick): lever operating ailerons and elevator

Cumulo-nimbus: towering, flat-based thunder-cloud

Cumulus: fluffy fine-weather cloud

Delta wing: triangular or near-triangular wing

Doppler: form of aircraft radar measuring speed over the ground

Drag: resistance caused by movement of body through the air

Ducted fan: wide-section, multi-bladed airscrew or impeller enclosed in annular ring or cowl

Elevator: moveable surface control

Fin: fixed vertical tail surface

Flap: device on trailing edge of wing to increase lift by increasing camber and/or wing area

Fuselage: central part of aeroplane

Glider: sailplane, unpowered plane

Glider tug: powered aeroplane used to tow glider to altitude

G-Suit: clothing worn by aircrew in high-performance aeroplanes

Gyrocopter (Autogiro): rotorcraft in which rotor freewheels. Forward thrust provided by propeller or jet

Hang-glider: simple glider in which control is achieved by changing position of pilot's body and thus moving centre of gravity

Helicopter: machine in which rotor or rotating wing gives lift

Helium: colourless, non-inflammable gas, lighter than air

Hydrogen: colourless, flammable gas, lighter than air

Hypersonic: speed much faster than that of sound

Instrument landing system (ILS): device used at all major airports to guide aircraft into line with runway and on to correct glide path

Inertial guidance: device based on gyroscope principle to indicate position of aircraft, lacking any external information

Inline engine: piston or reciprocating engine with cylinders arranged in fore and aft 'banks'

Jetliner: airliner with turbojet engine

Leading edge: front edge of aerofoil

Lift: force generated by aerofoil as it moves through the air

Mach number: system of relating air-speed to local speed of sound at a given altitude and temperature

Main plane (wing): primary lifting aerofoil of an aeroplane

Propeller: see also *Airscrew*: properly a 'pusher' airscrew mounted at rear of wing or fuselage

Prop-jet: aero engine where gas turbine turns an airscrew

Prototype: first model of any design

Radar: electronic means of establishing position, speed and track of moving objects

Radial engine: reciprocating (piston) engine with cylinders arranged like spokes around the crankcase

Roll: movement of aircraft about fore-and-aft (longitudinal) axis

Rotating wing (Rotor): rotating aerofoils providing lift

Rudder: moveable section of a vertical tail surface

Sideslip: sidesway, skid movement

Slat: moveable surface on leading edge of wing to smooth airflow at large angles of attack and delay onset of stall

Sound barrier: expression dating from time when it was thought that air would present impenetrable barrier to aircraft moving at the speed of sound

Spin: manoeuvre in which aeroplane descends vertically while rotating about its central axis

S.T.O.L.: short-take-off-and-landing

Stratosphere: part of atmosphere, lower limit 7 to 16km above earth's surface

Subsonic: less than speed of sound

Supersonic: faster than speed of sound

Swept wing: wing having centre line swept forward or backward

Swing wing (variable geometry): a moveable main aerofoil to combine characteristics of unswept wing with performance of highly swept wing

Tailplane: rear aerofoil or stabilizer

Thermal: 'bubble' of rising warm air

Thrust: measure of power of jet or rocket engine

Torque: reaction in opposite direction to rotation of airscrew or rotor

Trailing edge: rear edge of aerofoil

Troposphere: layer of atmosphere next to earth's surface

Turbofan: turbojet with large diameter ducted fan. Cold air driven rearwards surrounds hot gases, muffles noise

Turbojet: gas turbine engine deriving power from rearward thrust of high-velocity exhaust gases

Turn and bank indicator: instrument showing degree of bank, rate of turn, skid and slip

Variable geometry: see *Swing wing*

Variometer: instrument showing rate of climb or sink

Vectored thrust: variation of thrust line(s) usually by rotation of jet nozzles, to allow aeroplane to take off and land vertically

V.T.O.L.: vertical-take-off-and-landing

Yaw: movement of aircraft's nose about its vertical axis

Index

Answers to the quiz

1   Boeing B-17

2   The Canberra. It was built in the USA as the Martin B-57

3   It had swept wings with twin booms and an unswept tailplane

4   A triangular (or almost triangular) wing is called delta because its shape is like that of the fourth letter of the Greek alphabet

5   Multi Role Combat Aircraft – the swing-wing fighter bomber built for the RAF, the Luftwaffe and the Italian Aeronautica Militare

6   Supermarine Spitfire I and II and the Messerschmitt Me109

7   A noise insulation device to reduce the noise of existing jetliner engines

8   The Dornier Do-X flying boat of 1929 and the Convair B-36 intercontinental bomber

9   The B-36 was powered by a combination of six piston engines *and* four jets

10 The Messerschmitt Me 323 six-motor troop transport

11 Air Chief Marshal Sir Hugh Dowding

12 Reichsmarshall Hermann Goering

13 Douglas SBD-3 Dauntless

14 Junkers F.13 of 1919

15 They flew from Kitty Hawk in 1903

16 He was a famous German aeronaut who developed manned flight at the end of the nineteenth century

17 Orville Wright

18 Sir George Cayley. In 1853 he built the first man-carrying glider. The machine was flown by Sir George's coachman

19 He manoeuvres the glider in streams or bubbles of rising air

20 A thermal is a bubble of warm air rising from a heated surface. A thermalling pilot circles his glider within the bubble. A slope soaring pilot flies his glider back and forth in a wind stream blowing up the face of a hill

21 Cumulus are the fluffy white clouds which mark columns of rising air. Cumulo-nimbus clouds are the towering thunder storm clouds

22 By winch-tow and by aero-tow

23 The 747 has greater sweepback on all flying surfaces than the 707. Another feature of the 747 is the hump above the forward fuselage

24 It is designed to drop seven tons of water to help put out forest fires

25 Both machines were built almost entirely of wood

26 It is a long-range, very high speed (3,680km/hr) reconnaissance aircraft

27 Hendon is now the home of the RAF Museum

28 Sir Sydney Camm

29 It is a collection of historic aircraft, many of them in flying condition, based at Old Warden Aerodrome in Bedfordshire

30 The Zeppelin airships

31 Jason is the D H Cirrus Moth in which Amy Johnson flew solo from London to Darwin in 1930

32 The first manned vehicle (Apollo 11) touched down on the moon's surface

33 Vertical Take Off and Landing

34 The Hawker Siddeley Harrier GR Mk 1

35 The planform of the Tomcat can be changed in flight by varying the sweep of the wing

36 The tail rotor balances the torque or turning force of the main rotor. Otherwise the fuselage would rotate in the opposite direction

37 The Sikorsky R-4 which went into service in 1944

38 Short Take Off and Landing

39 It is a full size exact scale model of a projected aircraft. Mock-ups are usually built of wood

40 He presented the Schneider Trophy to be competed for by high-speed seaplanes

41 When the control column is pushed forward, the elevator goes down, creating an up force on the tail. This lowers the nose. Pulling back the control column raises the elevator and lifts the aircraft's nose

42 An automatic pilot system which can land an airliner safely in dense fog

43 The de Havilland DH82 Tiger Moth

44 Wilbur and Orville Wright

45 Frank Whittle

46 The Heinkel He178V1 which first flew on 27 August 1939

47 The Messerschmitt Me262

48 The de Havilland aircraft company. It was called the DH106 Comet

49 A fan-jet has a large diameter fan enclosed in a duct (a ducted fan) driven by a turbojet engine. The fan pushes large volumes of cold air around the jet engine providing thrust and blanketing the sound caused by the jet exhaust

50 The Junkers Ju87B. It was a single-engined low-wing monoplane with inverted-gull wings and a fixed undercarriage with large wheel fairings